Doyle and.

2·27·16

306·741·7550

On behalf of Millar College of the Bible, I acknowledge and thank Frank and Helen Rempel for their remarkable contribution to this ministry. There are certain key people who have left a significant mark on this ministry, and Frank and Helen are among them. Frank worked tirelessly both on campus and in the college community while also running his business and raising a family.

Phil Ruten, President, Millar College of the Bible

Frank Rempel seems kind of soft on missionaries like me. About ten years ago, he loaned us his big SUV to use in our summer travels, leaving himself to catch a ride to the office in his wife's car. In their apartment for missionaries, where we are spending the summer, hangs a beautiful wall decoration. It was given to the Rempels by the ambassador of a Muslim country who stayed in their home. Spending time with Frank has led me to do some soul-searching—how willing am I to go out on a limb for Jesus, the way this man does?

Doyle Klassen, Past President of Bibelschule Brake

My uncle and aunt, Frank and Helen Rempel, married young and grew to become a formidable team. They worked hard together, raised a large family by today's standards, and built a large company that has contributed to the local industry of the community and done humanitarian and missionary work throughout the world, far beyond what would normally be possible for a company the size of Rem Enterprises. That is true because of some of the basic values that Frank and Helen established early and have held to tenaciously throughout their lives. Each has very different gifts. Frank is the visionary and entrepreneur, and Helen has the supportive gift of administration and detail. The secret to their success in life—and they are the first to express it—is their love and commitment to God and their desire to spread the Good News as effectively as possible through their humanitarian enterprises, the witness of their lives, and direct verbal witness. You cannot spend more than half an hour with Frank without him expressing his passion for his work and his love for God.

Abe Funk, Past Executive Secretary of the
Baptist General Conference of Canada

Frank has a way of finding leaders and investing in them. He has a way of seeing ideas and pressing them into reality. He has confronted his personal need for a Savior and concluded that he would give of his life to help others enjoy the kind of relationship he enjoys with our Lord. Frank drives hard because he wants to make a difference. It means he has found his way to stand in a long list of gaps. I honor this man for his courage in the midst of many obstacles. I honor him for his humility before the Lord and his struggle to do right. I honor him for his desire to keep learning. I honor him because he actually lives his commitment to making disciples of Jesus Christ. I experienced his desire to see me grow in Christ, and I have watched him invite many to do the same.

Dwayne Uglem, President, Briercrest College and Seminary

About Our
FATHER'S
BUSINESS

An Autobiography

FRANK REMPEL
WITH MARTIN M. CULY

Printed in Canada

ISBN: 978-1-4866-1213-0 (paperback)
ISBN: 978-1-4866-1212-3 (casebound)

Word Alive Press
131 Cordite Road, Winnipeg, MB R3W 1S1
www.wordalivepress.ca

MIX
Paper from
responsible sources
FSC® C016245

Cataloguing in Publication information may be obtained through Library and Archives Canada.

PREFACE   vii

I The Rempel Heritage   1
II Maria Teichroeb   5
III My Early Years   11
IV Helen   29
V Farmhand, Cowboy, and Hobo   33
VI A New Life   41
VII Learning to Trust and to Give   47
VIII From Journeyman to Businessman   55
IX The Christian Service Brigade   63
X Bible College Student   67
XI Following God's Call   71
XII About Our Father's Business   81
XIII The Marriage of Business and Ministry   87
XIV Family, Business, and Ministry   95
XV Adventures in Flying   99
XVI Back to Millar   105
XVII The 1990s: New Ministries, New Milestones   115
XVIII Ministering to the Nations   121
XIX Rem: All These Things Shall Be Added Unto You   137
XX A Decade of Adventure, Discipline and Growth   145
XXI A New Millenium and New Beginnings   157

EPILOGUE   161

APPENDIX 1:
Have You Made the Most Important Choice of Your Life?   163
APPENDIX 2:
Have You Made the Wonderul Discovery of the Spirit-Filled Life?   169

Preface

I am grateful not only to the Lord for His faithfulness over the years but also to a number of people who have helped put the pieces together for this book. I want to thank Abe Funk, whose research into our family history serves as the basis for the first chapter. My daughter Leann provided valuable assistance in typing the initial notes for this book. I am particularly grateful to my wife, Helen, for her patience, encouragement, and willingness to help nurture this project along.

The overarching goal of this book is to highlight the importance of recognizing that Jesus is the Vine and we are merely branches. He is our source of strength, wisdom, and direction for yesterday, today, and forever. Helen and I have had the privilege of being branches of the Vine for most of our lives. We have sought to abide in the Vine so that we could bear much fruit, one day at a time, with the "talent" God entrusted to us. It has been our hope that we might leave a legacy for generations to follow as we all await the time when the Vine and the branches will be united in eternity together.

Frank Rempel
January 2013

When Frank Rempel was told in 2008 that Briercrest College and Seminary would like to award him an honorary doctorate for his faithful and fruitful service to the Lord over the years, his response was consistent with his typical approach to life: "If I am getting a degree, I had better take some courses." He immediately signed up for several of the New Testament courses I taught at Briercrest Seminary. The Lord connected our hearts, as only He can, right from the first day we met, and we have had many rich times of fellowship and a number of memorable adventures together in the years since. My wife, Jo-Anna, and I are both very grateful to the Lord for the special times we have had with Frank and Helen, including spending extended periods of time with them on their farm. Reminiscing with both of them about their experiences over the years as we worked on this book has been a delight. Though health challenges have certainly begun to slow them both down, they continue to be a shining example of a couple who lives for Jesus day by day. May we all run the race of life so well.

Martin Culy
January 2013

CHAPTER I

The Rempel Heritage

A good name is more desirable than great riches; to be esteemed is better than silver or gold...Humility and the fear of the LORD bring wealth and honor and life (Proverbs 22:1–4).

Each of our lives is shaped by a variety of factors. We are all born with a distinct personality—one that cannot be predicted and that sometimes seems to be forced on our unsuspecting parents. We are also a product of our experiences—and not only our own, but also the experiences of those who raise us. Much of who I am today and many of the things I hold dear flow naturally out of the challenges my parents faced as immigrants to a new land. They, in turn, had been shaped by their earlier experiences and the experiences of their parents. This is the story of God's patient work in my life, even before I knew Him, and how He taught me to increasingly depend on Him—as a branch depends on the Vine to live and bear fruit. My story, though, begins with the Rempel story.

In those days, riverboat builders began the construction process by building the keel of the boat first. It had to be strong enough to handle the rough conditions of river travel—including colliding with the occasional floating log and other flotsam and jetsam—and to bear the weight of the whole boat when it was transported on land using rollers. One early keel builder was a man who came to be known as "Rempel." Some have speculated that this nickname came from the loud rumbling ("rempeling") sounds the boat made as it was pulled over the rollers. Others have suggested that a "rumple" in Holland was a bump in the road. Whatever the origin of the name, the quality of this man's work gave dignity to the name Rempel, which was to become his family name.

The first Rempel recorded actually dates back to the year 1250, to the city of Pfullingen, south of Reutlingen, in southern Germany. Some of the Rempels lived in the area where Peter Waldo, one of the earliest Reformers, had many followers who came to be known as Waldensians. The Waldensians looked to the Bible as the only source of authority and rejected the authority and many of the teachings of the Roman Catholic Church. They lived a simple life, serving the Lord and others—a life devoted to the teachings of the New Testament. Their "radical" beliefs led to strong persecution from the civil authorities for not following the state church. As the persecution intensified in southern Germany and Switzerland, many of these believers moved north.

In northwest Germany in the city of Bremen, Herr Friedrichs von Rempel was born in 1384. He served in the army under King Sigismund from 1416 to 1420 in the conquest of Bohemia, which is now the Czech Republic, near Breclav. It is likely that shortly after this period some of the Rempels settled in Moravia. Later, in 1525, there is evidence that some of the Rempel families followed the radical Reformer Hans Hut, who had many followers. Hut, who had been heavily influenced by the teachings of Thomas Müntzer, was an early Anabaptist (Wiedertäufer). The Anabaptists received their name from their practice of insisting that those who had been baptized as infants must be baptized again when they became followers of Jesus Christ. As persecution of the Anabaptists became increasingly severe, they sought out a safer place to live. They traveled north in wagon trains to the Free City of Danzig (now Gdańsk, Poland) and the city of Elbing, Poland, on the delta of the Vistula River. There they found a safe haven where the government allowed them to practice their faith freely.

In either the first wagon train of 1535 or the second wagon train of 1604, the Rempel clan entered a new era. When they settled in northern

Poland, they became part of another Anabaptist movement known as the Mennonites. The Mennonites were committed pacifists, separated themselves from the larger society to live their own distinct lifestyle, carefully followed the teachings of the New Testament, and understood conversion as embracing Jesus Christ as Lord of their lives. Records dating to 1673 show that Rempel families were members of the Mennonite church in Danzig at that time.

In the year 1789, one Rempel family decided to move to the Ukraine with a group of other families. They wanted to homestead where the ruling queen of Russia, Catherine the Great, had offered free land for experienced farmers. They traveled down the Dnieper River valley until they came to Chortitza Island and the city of Zaporizhzhya on the east side of the river. There they settled on the west side of the river, where Bernhard Rempel I was born in 1799 in the village of Kosholski, also known as the Old Mennonite Colony or Chortitza.

In this new land they found rich, fertile soil and a mild climate. Here they could grow fruit trees and many other crops, including cereal grains, and they soon began to prosper. First they built their own farm machinery and other equipment. Later they improved their prospects by building steam-powered shops so they could manufacture their products for sale. By the latter part of the 1850s, it is estimated that the colonies were building 15 percent of all farm machinery in the Ukraine.

Though they prospered, the Rempel family remained very conservative and separated in their lifestyle, living in their own eight villages in the Chortitza area, with a small acreage for each family. They had gardens and milk cows and were self-sufficient, with their own German schools.

THE REMPELS COME TO CANADA
God blessed them and said to them, "Be fruitful and increase in number; fill the earth and subdue it" (Genesis 1:28)

Bernhard Rempel I and his life partner, Helen Neufeld, were married on September 1, 1818, in Kosholski, Ukraine. They had eleven children. Their sixth child, Bernhard Rempel II, was born on March 31, 1828, at 7:00 a.m. His father passed away when he was only eleven years old. At the age of twenty-one, on October 1, 1849, Bernhard II married Anna

3

Peters, and they had ten children together. As his father had done before him, Bernhard named his sixth child after himself. Bernhard Rempel III was born on December 22, 1860, at 9:00 a.m.

In the "old country," the Russian czar had demanded that everyone become citizens, attend state schools, learn the Russian language, serve in the military, and meet all the other demands placed on citizens. As Mennonites, however, the Rempels were pacifists, very conservative, and equally independent. Rather than fighting for their rights, they once again began looking for a new land where they would have the freedom to live as they had always lived. And so when Bernard III was fifteen years old he moved with his father to southern Manitoba in Canada. The Rempels had enjoyed ninety-five years in Southern Ukraine, a land flowing with milk and honey. Now they began settling in a land with a much harsher climate on the prairies of Canada.

Although this overview of the early Rempel family history is quite brief due to the limited nature of the records available, it sheds important light on family traits that I now recognize as part of my own DNA. I come from a long line of Anabaptists who have for centuries been staunchly committed to serving the Lord Jesus Christ and following the teachings of the Bible. I come from a long line of pioneers who were willing to homestead. I come from a long line of entrepreneurs, people who could start with very little and through hard work and innovation make a good life for themselves. I come from a long line of nonconformists, men and women who were willing to stand against the tide, even at great cost to themselves. I come from a long line of survivors, men and women who somehow found a way to continue the family line and prosper even when the odds were against them. And I come from a long line of men and women who have been blessed by our Heavenly Father, whom they gladly served and worshipped.

CHAPTER II

Maria Teichroeb

Her husband is respected at the city gate, where he takes his seat among the elders of the land. She makes linen garments and sells them, and supplies the merchants with sashes. She is clothed with strength and dignity; she can laugh at the days to come. She speaks with wisdom, and faithful instruction is on her tongue. She watches over the affairs of her household and does not eat the bread of idleness. Her children arise and call her blessed; her husband also, and he praises her: "Many women do noble things, but you surpass them all." Charm is deceptive, and beauty is fleeting; but a woman who fears the LORD is to be praised. Give her the reward she has earned, and let her works bring her praise at the city gate (Proverbs 31:23–31).

Although my mother, Maria Teichroeb, was not born a Rempel, she was cut from the same mold. Her father, David Teichroeb, was the son of Ukrainian immigrants, Daniel (1835–1891) and Margaret (Braun) Teichroeb. David married Elizabeth Goertzen, and they lived in Hoffstadt, several miles northeast of Altona, Manitoba. Maria was born there on April 26, 1888, the sixth of eight children, but she was not the daughter of David Teichroeb. All that is known of Maria's father is that he was some Frenchman who was passing through the area and got her mother pregnant. There is no record of the circumstances surrounding the pregnancy or where the Frenchman came from.

The news of the pregnancy was, of course, a big scandal in the very conservative Mennonite community. The scandal, though, was the least of young Maria's problems. When she was only two years old her mother died. Her father married again, but when Maria was just five years old he disowned her and put her in the care of neighbors, the Funk family. From age five to nine, Maria essentially lived as a slave of this family and was frequently mistreated. I recall a story she told me from her years with the Funks:

> The woman of the house, Mrs. Funk, discovered that something she regarded as valuable was missing from her room. When she accused me, I told her, "I didn't take it." But she severely beat me anyway until finally, in order to stop the beating, I "admitted" that I had taken it. To my horror I was beaten again because I had not admitted what I had done soon enough! Later, Mrs. Funk heard her own son confess that he was the one who had taken the valuable item and that I was not guilty.
>
> A few days after this, a neighbor lady came along and saw me limping and trying to keep up with my work. "Why are you limping?" she asked. I replied, "My sores are not healing." I had been beaten so badly with a strap that a wound between my legs was festering in an open sore. At that point, the neighbor intervened and I was able to go and live with the Wiebe family.

The rest of Maria's childhood was spent in a much more typical family situation. Although she had faced severe trials as a young child, remarkably they did not destroy her or make her bitter. She seems to have been born with a tough pioneering spirit, and the trials only tempered her strength and brought out a loving and courageous personality that was respected and admired by those who knew her.

BERNHARD IV AND MARIA

Blessed is the man who does not walk in the counsel of the wicked or stand in the way of sinners or sit in the seat of mockers. But his delight is in the law of the LORD, and on his law he meditates day and night. He is like a tree planted by streams of water, which yields its fruit in season and whose leaf does not wither. Whatever he does prospers (Psalm 1:1–3).

In her teen years, Maria met my father, Bernhard Rempel IV. He had been born in Manitoba in 1885, ten years after his parents settled in the Mennonite colony there, and was known to be both bright and handsome. He soon proved to also be very wise. After meeting Maria, my father remarked, "This Maria Teichroeb is very attractive to me." He quickly recognized her as the most wonderful, caring, and healthy wife a man could ask for. When he decided to move to Rhineland, Saskatchewan, in 1906, Maria found a family needing someone to do housework in the area and took the job to be near him. A year later, on December 15, 1907, they were married in Rhineland Church and moved in with Bernhard's family.

Maria Teichroeb, 1906

Bernhard Rempel IV, 1927

Their early life together was very prosperous. Although Bernhard and Maria lived with his family initially, that very first winter he established his own twenty-eight-acre homestead. On October 24, 1908, their first son was born, Bernhard Rempel V; and over the next ten years their family grew to include six children and their farm prospered.

By 1918, they had built an eight-room house. They had a huge barn that included a long hallway connecting the barn to the house, a new well that was over 100 feet deep and produced lots of good drinking water, and a cistern to ensure they always had plenty of water. There was a pump jack system (instead of a windmill), a big garden, and fifteen horses. Wheat, their main crop, was selling for nine dollars a bushel at the time. Life was good, and by 1922 two more children had been added to the family.

In our early years on the farm, my father decided to buy a new tractor, a Case 12–20. With its astounding twelve horsepower it could pull a plow with three shares. My father then built a blacksmith shop where he could sharpen and shape his own plowshares. What he was really building, though, was a life for his family. Bernhard V, my oldest brother, who was now in his early teen years, became an expert horseman and was a big help to my father with the fieldwork. The family was healthy and thriving, and things were going very well; but dark clouds were on the horizon that would drastically change their lives forever.

1923 Model 12-20 Case Tractor

By 1924, the elders of the colonies had begun noticing that their culture was beginning to erode. The first World War (1914–1918) was behind them, but their way of life was being threatened by new rules and regulations, and the language of the colony (German), in particular, was being challenged. As pacifists, rather than resisting the emerging pressure to change their ways, the elders began making plans to relocate the colony.

My grandfather, Bernard Rempel III, supported this plan, but the same cannot be said of my father. Bernard Rempel IV had already become an independent thinker by that time, and much to the dismay of many, when my grandfather began setting things in motion to uproot his farm and move to Mexico, my father was quick to tell everyone, "I'm not moving to Mexico. I'm staying here!" He didn't realize at the time what this decision would mean for his family and his farm. He soon discovered that the colony villages and all of their land would all be sold as a single block of property. This meant that he would not able to keep the land he had so carefully developed or the buildings he had built with his own two hands, since by deed it was all part of the colony holdings.

Bernard Rempel V, 1936

This was a difficult blow, but the final outcome was even worse. The sale of the property was handled by chosen trustees, who unfortunately were bribed by an unscrupulous land company. In the end, they signed over the title to the whole property without the colony receiving any cash whatsoever. While the supposed sale was in process, my father had raised another crop and had a significant amount of grain put away in storage, but as a result of the "sale" my father lost all of his land and all of the grain he had worked so hard to grow as well. His beautiful farm, the best in the village, was now gone. He received nothing at all for his property.

But my father was not quite as pacifistic in his thinking as the rest of the colony, and he proceeded to hire a lawyer. In the end, though, it was a battle that could not be won. He soon found himself not only in debt but also without any support whatsoever from his father, relatives, or friends, all of whom were staunch pacifists and would not fight for their rights or for their property. Ultimately, he was forced to give up. The loss of the colony property became the biggest land swindle in the history of Saskatchewan, and my father went broke. With nothing left to his name, he had no other option but to move onto a rented farm in 1926.

CHAPTER III

My Early Years

Do you not know that in a race all the runners run, but only one gets the prize? Run in such a way as to get the prize. Everyone who competes in the games goes into strict training. They do it to get a crown that will not last; but we do it to get a crown that will last forever. Therefore I do not run like a man running aimlessly; I do not fight like a man beating the air. No, I beat my body and make it my slave so that after I have preached to others, I myself will not be disqualified for the prize (1 Corinthians 9:24–27).

As my mother tells the story, the first snowstorm of 1924 came on October 12, and I, their sixth and youngest son, was close behind. After that, she was fond of saying, it seemed like it never quit being stormy around our house! My older brothers were all quiet and resourceful and always got along well. No one quite knows what happened with me! My extremely active personality was apparent from the very beginning and has never changed.

My older sister tells a story from my early years: "I was babysitting Frank, but Frank was too lively and too loud. So I made Frank sit on the top step of the cellar stairway, and before closing the door I told him, 'The tiger will not know you are here if you sit very quiet.'" It was dark and cold, and for the remainder of that day I apparently gave my sister no more trouble! As I got older, when I would cause problems with my younger sisters my mother would tell me, "Go find your father, and stay with him!" Thankfully, my father never seemed bothered by my personality, but I talked a lot and he didn't, and he would occasionally tell me to shut up.

The rented farm where my parents had been forced to resettle with their ten children after twenty wonderful and prosperous years on the homestead was eight miles south of the village of Rhineland. For a young boy the world was still full of potential. In the large garden of approximately two acres, I was kept busy helping to raise vegetables: potatoes, corn, beans, carrots, cabbage, sunflower seeds, and gooseberries. The combination of fertile land, good cultivation, and meticulous weeding resulted in plenty of vegetables. Between the vegetables and our milk cows, chickens, and hogs, we were well fed in our early years there.

In the fall, three or four large hogs would be butchered with help from our neighbors. This annual event brought with it a big party atmosphere, as we butchered the hogs, rendered the lard, cleaned the intestines, made sausage, and smoked the sausage all in one day. This event also provided cured meat for the long winter months. I have many pleasant memories from those years.

Although my father always worked extremely hard, it was also clear that a lot depended on my mother. I can still remember seeing her busy in the summer kitchen for hours on end at the big cookstove with the long cooking surface.

Some of my earliest memories are happy recollections of how privileged I felt to go with my father into his blacksmith shop. The year was 1928, and as I watched my father heat plowshares red hot on his hearth, where the coals were kept extra hot by blowing air into the flames, I stretched as tall as I could to turn the crank to blow more air into the flames as my father added a second plowshare to heat. A pair of tongs were used to lay the hot plowshare on the anvil, and the tip was then quickly shaped and then sharpened with a one-hand hammer. The sharpened share was immediately "quenched" in a mixture of oil and water. Early experiences in my father's blacksmith shop led to a fascination with shaping metal that became a driving force in my life and set me on an adventure of learning much more about working with metal in my early years. Throughout those years my father also regularly taught me to repair machinery of all sorts, and this helped stimulate later ideas for designing new machinery.

One of my favorite activities in my early years was to play in the trees near our garden and house. There was a wonderful hiding place in the trees where it was very difficult for anyone to find me, especially adults. I remember being delighted during the windy summer months that the wind could not reach me when I was inside the trees. I also enjoyed late summer when the berries ripened. Some of our neighbors would often go after dark to eat berries in the big garden that belonged to Jacob Funk. I have to confess that I told them about those berries! When Jake Funk discovered that his berries were being pilfered, he began standing watch so that he could chase away whoever was sneaking into his garden. One night, when some of the boys went on a berry hunt to his garden, I quietly followed them with a friend. As they began picking berries, we started making all sorts of noise to make it sound like Jake Funk was coming to get them. We stomped our feet and even lit a match for good measure. Those berry thieves took off as fast as they could run, and we chased them for a while to make sure they were good and scared. A couple of them ended up running into a mesh fence. Fortunately, there were no serious injuries…at least, not until they found out who had been chasing them!

Springtime had come to the farm in southwest Saskatchewan. The spring runoff was over, the breezes were warm, the grass was slowly starting to grow, and the crocus flowers were out in full dress. It was time to get the three bottoms (three-share plow) ready; the plowing would soon begin. My older brothers were getting the drill ready, and the harness for the four-horse team had been oiled and repaired. The 12–20 Case tractor was carefully checked over, and the bearings were adjusted. Everything was ready to go.

Mother told me, "Go with Dad to haul wheat to the McMahon elevator. We need supplies." McMahon was four miles east of our farm, and the two-hour trip to town with my father was one of my favorite things to do when I was young, particularly if my dad allowed me to spend five cents to buy three chocolate bars! While we were in town, we would also typically pick up the mail with the *Winnipeg Free Press* magazine and stop to buy yeast and salt. My dad always called me Fritz in those days. In fact, that was my nickname until my teen years.

On this particular occasion, my father had hitched on two Percheron workhorses to the grain wagon after carefully putting axle grease on the wagon wheel hubs. Backing up to the granary, the horses stood patiently while we loaded the wagon with fifty bushels. My father used a half-bushel scoop to load the wagon. I helped with a small pail.

When we were about halfway home we met an automobile going in the opposite direction. It was Mr. Sawatsky, our local store owner, who was on his way home after loading up with supplies in Swift Current. As soon as we stopped, he got out of his truck and came to meet us with a huge watermelon in his hands. "Mr. Rempel," he said, "I've got a good deal for you, and you need this for your big family."

"How much?" Father asked.

"You take it home," he responded, "and weigh it. Then, next time you're in town, we'll agree on a price and you can pay me then. You're a very honest man and always pay your bills. So you can weigh it yourself and tell me the weight when you come to town again."

My father took the watermelon. When we got home we discovered that it weighed nearly thirty pounds! My mother baked a huge batch of Rollkuchen (deep fried biscuits), and we proceeded to eat them along with the whole melon. What a feast it was! I learned a simple lesson that day: it pays to be honest and have a good name (and credit) so you can eat watermelon! This incident had a lasting effect on me and was the beginning of developing my own value system, which would serve me well later in life. My father was known as a gentleman who dressed well, worked hard, and always kept his word. He was a man of integrity, and that is what I wanted to be too.

There was a good crop that year. My father had a new Case threshing machine, 22-inch, I believe. He traded in the 12–20 Case tractor for a new Model L Case tractor, also on steel wheels, but much improved. It was the biggest Case gas-powered tractor available, and it would allow him to rent and work more land several miles to the northeast. There was optimism in the air, and life was very busy with eleven children, six boys and five girls.

Three years had now gone by since my family had moved to the small village of Hamburg, and we were mixed farming on rented land. The one major purchase at this time was a 1923 Ford Model T sedan. It had a two-speed transmission and could travel at the unthinkable speed of twenty-five miles per hour! It was now possible to travel to Swift Current in one hour, do some shopping, and come home, all in one day! My first trip with my father was very exciting. We walked on the sidewalk, went to the Cooper General Store, and ate ice cream. Going to church meant that the Model T had to be started on a cold morning using a crank fastened at the front of the engine. My older brothers got plenty of exercise spinning the crank; the faster they would spin it, the better the chance it would start.

Years later, Dad bought a Pontiac with a six-volt battery that had enough power to start the engine with no cranking required. I discovered that the power came when you put a connection from the positive side of the battery to the self-starter. When we stepped on the starter button, the engine would start. The lesson for me was that it is a lot more fun to be positive and a self-starter than to be a crank!

One of the things I truly appreciated about my parents was the effort they put into making Christmas celebrations special for the whole family. There were always plenty of gifts for everyone, especially candy and nuts (particularly peanuts). Family and friends would gather together, and we children would have a wonderful time playing together. One Christmas day, when I was about five or six years old, I was given a gift in a big basket. When I looked inside, I found the expected nuts and candy and also a Meccano set: nuts and bolts and pieces of steel with holes in them that could be bolted together. My older brother added a box of Erector Set pieces, strips of metal that would make my Meccano set much larger. This was the best present I could have possibly received. Designing and bolting pieces together soon became a regular part of my winter months at home and also helped to both feed and stimulate my appetite for building things. A spring-powered clock motor allowed me to build machines with moving parts. In the summers, I would put aside the Meccano set and build with wood, or anything else I could get my hands on.

Another Christmas some of our cousins made a particularly memorable arrival at our home. They had converted a sedan car body into a sleigh! The engine and engine housing had been removed, and lines to control the horses had been fed through a slot in the firewall. We children were especially excited to see this amazing contraption arrive at our house, pulled by two horses, with six children and two parents inside! They spent the night with us, and boy, did we have a good time, playing games and eating a lot of good Christmas food—ham, moose, pies, peanuts, and candy. The weather was very cold, as could be expected on the prairies at that time of year, but our hearts were warm.

—1930—

Though the fig tree does not bud and there are no grapes on the vines, though the olive crop fails and the fields produce no food, though there are no sheep in the pen and no cattle in the stalls, yet I will rejoice in the LORD, I will be joyful in God my Savior (Habakkuk 3:17–18).

The wind kept on blowing, the tumbleweeds were pulling against the fence line, and there was a cloud of dust in the air. It was the beginning of a long series of events and struggles—the Great Depression. Even as a six-year-old, I noticed a change taking place. My father showed signs of stress, something that I had not noticed before. It was brought about by the crash in the stock market, which had a dramatic effect on the price of wheat, among other things.

We began to lose precious machinery that had been bought on time but could no longer be paid for. I sensed uncertainty in my family; my brother Peter had health problems, and there was not a strong sense of spiritual grounding in the family. The tough years had begun.

During this time, when I was seven or eight years old, I designed and built a small bean-thrashing (threshing) machine. It consisted of a roller with spikes to shred the ripe bean pod and a blower to blow the shredded pods away like straw. The beans would end up in a pile on the floor of the shed. It saved a lot of time, since shredding by hand, one pod at a time, was incredibly slow and tedious. The thrasher was powered by a flat belt around a large flywheel, which had a handle, like a crank, that my two younger sisters had to take turns cranking while I fed the thrasher. It was quite a job to convince them to cooperate, but eventually their curiosity got the better of them. My next project was building a small plow and a large toy wooden tractor, which also required girl power to run. I, of course, served as the supervisor!

Around the age of nine or ten, I built a treadle-powered lathe with my brother Peter. I would work the treadle while Peter machined baseball bats and other items. One year, we found an old go-cart, a geared, hand-powered speedy contraption. We spent a lot of time rebuilding it because we planned to work it much harder than the original builders had intended. This helped us to get around the farm much faster than we could walk. To make some money, my brother and I raised potatoes, and my father let us use the Model T Ford to take our potatoes to Swift Current and sell them.

THE DEPRESSION

What my parents didn't know when they moved our family to the rented farm was that the challenges had only just begun. When the stock market crashed in 1929, the first thing affected was the price of wheat, which dropped to as low as twenty-nine cents a bushel, down from nine dollars a bushel just a few years earlier. Later, the rain would stop coming and grasshoppers would begin eating our crops. The heavy financial losses during those Great Depression years were a tremendous burden to my parents. The deep depression they experienced at times was only compounded by the lack of spiritual joy, love, and peace in their hearts.

My father and mother had both tried to adapt to the beliefs of the Summerfelder Mennonite congregation that they now belonged to. Their integrity, open and honest lifestyle, and commitment to God and their family were strong. Their relationship with others was peaceful, and they firmly embraced a strong, disciplined work ethic with great enthusiasm.

At times, this brought pain to my father when he had to depend on fellow members of the congregation. He found that many let him down, and some neighbors that he should have been able to trust were deceptive. I remember sensing this struggle as I listened to conversations between my parents. I also came to realize that their Summerfelder teachers were telling them that they could not know if they would go to heaven when they died; they could only work hard and hope they might make it. This kind of thinking didn't do them much good as they faced the challenges of the Depression.

I wanted to help my father. After all, he was my hero and very important to me. But how could I help? What could I do? The Depression years increasingly took a toll on him, and I sensed that the ambition that had always driven him was no longer there. At first, he responded with frustration, particularly as he was faced with a "no crop" year. When the soil began drifting, he realized that plowing the land in the spring was not the best approach to farming. So he bought a Cockshutt eight-foot one-way disk, with a seeder box attachment on top. This single-operation seeding process immensely improved the ability to stop soil drifting and also saved time. Furthermore, horses were no longer required in the spring seeding operation.

Father persevered, trying his best through the 1930s to keep us together. We younger children helped Mother by getting the sunflower stalks ready for fuel. Pressed cattle manure and horse droppings made a quick fire and provided heat to make fine *paankuchen* (thin pancakes or crepes), which we ate with a berry sauce from plums or currants. It took a lot of paankuchen to feed twelve or thirteen people! But Mother always seemed to know how to do it.

Off to School

My strong relationship with my mother began very young. She was a very disciplined person and never seemed to give much thought to her own problems. Her focus was always on encouraging others. It was her constant encouragement that made me willing to do all I could to help in the garden, with cooking, and doing chores. We had some milk cows, and one of my chores was separating the milk from the cream. When the cream can was filled we would ship it to Swift Current by train for cash sales.

When I turned seven years old it was time for school. My first few months were spent at a nearby German school. I was part of a very small group who were mostly learning to read and study a catechism. On the first day of school, my older brother John had a little talk with me. "You'll have to look after yourself at school," he told me. Sure enough, on that very first day an overweight boy began saying bad things about me and taunting me. I remembered what my brother had told me and quickly hit him in the face as hard as I could. He went away crying but came after me later at recess. I gave him another one in the face, and this time he left me alone.

When I got home, my brother asked me how my first day of school had gone. I calmly informed him that I had only had two fights, both with the same boy. He responded, "You know, I've been going to school for a few years now and never once had a fight." That got me thinking. Perhaps looking after myself didn't mean fighting! I would have to try harder to get along.

When I was almost eight years old I was sent to a different school. There it became even clearer that I still had a lot to learn about relating to others, but growing in this area was difficult when winning at every activity was my goal, and being number one in my studies came next.

The school was two miles from our home, and in the warm months I would run all the way. The fact that I could get to school faster than my siblings encouraged me to push myself hard and grow in strength. In the winter months, my older siblings would take us younger ones to school in a bobsleigh covered with lots of blankets to keep us warm.

In those early school years, some of the older boys wanted to smoke but couldn't afford the tobacco. So they would bring cigarette paper to school, pack it with dry leaves or grass, and try to smoke it. Sometimes they even added a bit of dried horse manure. You could smell it a mile away. I was intrigued by smoking, like most young boys, but not so intrigued by putting dried leaves in my mouth, and certainly not interested in adding horse manure. At home, one of my older brothers tried smoking dried leaves, but this produced too much fire and led to a lot of coughing. It made no sense to me at all. So I never tried it myself, but I do remember trying chewing tobacco at one point. It cost ten cents. I took one bite of that stuff, got sick, and decided chewing tobacco was no better than dried leaves or manure.

A new teacher came to the school when I was ten years old. His name was Mr. Jacob Neufeld, and he was a Christian who showed us love and taught us Christian values. He quickly became my favorite teacher. Through his encouragement I began striving to excel in my studies. I gained in confidence and came to enjoy learning for the first time. (I would eventually read through all of the books in the school library, which were not too many but covered all of the material for all eight grades.) Mr. Neufeld taught us how to sing—alto, bass, tenor, and soprano—and we sang a lot, new songs and Christian songs. He also taught us how to treat one another with love, and the atmosphere in our one-room school house of twenty to twenty-five students dramatically improved. When he offered a prize for learning Scripture my interest was captured. Here was another competition! Although Bible memorization would later become a very important part of my life, at this point memorizing the Gospel of John was simply a way of winning a New Testament.

Frank visits with his teacher, Jacob Neufeld, 1995

Another important competition that began at that time involved fastball (a faster version of slow-pitch softball). My three brothers— George, John, and Peter—and I enjoyed playing fastball to win prizes on field days. I thrived on being number one in all areas: in drama, in class, in track and field, and in fastball; and when the teacher's very pretty niece came to live with them, I made certain that I was number one on her list too! Her name was Hilda, and she was two years older than I was. Unfortunately for me, after only two years she moved away.

We were still in the middle of the Depression as my teenage years approached. In my early years, I had been very attached to my father. He had taught me many things, like working in the blacksmith shop, repairing harnesses, and riding our favorite horse, Fly. Fly could run like the wind and won a number of prizes. I would run her full tilt every chance I got. My father had taught me how to herd cattle out of the pasture and then watch them as they grazed on roadsides to keep them away from the seeded crops.

Riding the horse during the summer months and looking after livestock was a highlight of my childhood. But as the Depression and drought lingered on, my father became much quieter and more remote, and my mother gave me more attention. She let me sleep alone in my own bed, where I would not be pestered by my older brother any longer. She taught me that I had to show love to my brothers and not fight constantly. She told me about the importance of keeping myself pure sexually and not indulging in dirty, immoral acts. She said, "You are growing, and you have a bright, healthy mind and body. Keep herself pure, and you will remain healthy and well." I know that it was due to my mother's forthright encouragement and God's grace that I was able to stay away from sexual impurity and save myself for my wife, Helen.

Teen Years

In my early teen years, my parents allowed my two older brothers and me to spend several days at Lac Pelletier. Mother prepared food for us, and we loaded up the Model T and set out for the lake. We caught and ate perch—it seemed like a hundred of them!—and spent the rest of the days swimming, diving, and boating, and we slept under the stars. We returned home tired and sunburned, but very happy.

As the decade of drought continued, in 1938, at the age of fourteen, I went with my father and brother George to Coaldale, Alberta, in midsummer. We traveled for more than a day on a gravel highway and got a job pitching loose sweet clover hay. There was no crop to harvest on our farm that year, and my father, brother, and I worked very hard together to earn some cash.

I started grade 8 that year with just one other student in my class. Not surprisingly, I soon became very bored. When I turned fifteen years old that October, it was only a matter of weeks before I decided that I had had enough school for now. The trapping season, which ran from November to February, had started, and I was too busy trapping weasels to go to school. Weasel skins brought in cash, which was hard to come by.

I remember the teacher coming to visit my mother and father. He was to the point: "I checked Frank's records. He graduated from grade 7 with the highest marks ever recorded. You should send Frank to high school." My father said that he was pleased that I had learned well, but high school was too far away to be practical. Although I was more than happy to go along with my father's wishes at the time, I would later regret not making the effort to go to high school.

Besides trapping weasels that year, I also repaired the old saddle, which had broken from rough usage. When I took the saddle apart, the wooden "tree" seemed totally ruined. I decided it needed a partial steel frame, so I found a piece of flat iron and heated up the forge in the blacksmith shop. When the iron was red hot, I shaped it to fit the saddle. I then drilled a hole for a good-size bolt, which became the base of the saddle horn. No one else believed the saddle could be fixed, which of course only motivated me more! I informed everyone that it was going to be a roping saddle when I was finished with it. Using pieces of tin to hold the broken pieces of wood together, I bolted the steel to the wooden frame, put the leather covering back on, and fashioned a saddle horn that looked better than the original. To test the strength, I put the saddle on the workhorse, tied a rope to the saddle horn, and pulled a sled full of manure out of the barn. The saddle stayed together!

Frank's homemade roping saddle, 1941

My oldest brother, Ben, who was married and had his own farm by that time, said, "I'd like to buy that saddle. I always liked it." When I told him I didn't know what it was worth, he said he would give me twenty dollars for it. Twenty dollars! That was more money than I could imagine, but I gladly accepted it and then used it to buy enough material to build two more saddles. By making saddles, trapping weasels, and starting a fur-trading business with my neighbor's boys (who didn't have trapper's licenses and thus needed someone to act as a middleman to sell their furs), I began learning the art of how to make a profit. I also began to desire to have my own business with lots of employees one day. The point was not to have a large business for my own ego; having experienced the challenges of the Great Depression I sincerely wanted to help others find employment.

In those days, you often had to be willing to travel to find work. Early one morning in May of 1940, my brother George and I, along with two older men, set out in our Model A sedan for Barnwell, Alberta, a village near Taber. We met with a farmer there who was looking for help thinning out his sugar beet crop and agreed on a price per acre for his whole crop of forty acres. For accommodations, we were allowed to stay in the beet shack and given a supply of potatoes to eat.

After sweeping it out and storing our clothes, we went to buy additional groceries: bread, jam, bologna, and oatmeal. We also purchased a beet hoe for each of us and a file to keep the hoes sharp. For the job before us, we needed to shorten the handles on the hoes down to twenty-four inches and then use an anvil, chisel, and hammer to cut off the square corners of the blade to make long, thin corners. This would make it easier to slice between the young beet plants.

As we worked, we would pull some of the plants with our left hands, while our right hands held the hoe. We would then use the hoe to clear a space, leaving about eight inches between the remaining young sugar beet plants. The rows were thick with sugar beet plants, and it was hard work to leave only one plant by itself. At age sixteen, I was quite agile, but my muscles quickly became very sore from bending over.

The days were long and very tiring. We took turns taking time off to cook lunch, but my first attempt at cooking did not endear me to the others! First, the wood-burning cookstove seemed intent on sending off billows of smoke. Then, the potatoes I was cooking turned green and didn't look very appetizing. In hindsight, I guess it wasn't a good idea to mix green vegetables in with the potatoes!

The hard work and challenges of living in the beet shack were offset by the income we were making. We were earning between four and five dollars per day according to our calculations, which was about double the daily labor rate at the time. But I found myself not fitting in very well with the others. One day I was cooking oatmeal for lunch when I discovered it was full of worms. It made me feel sick when I realized that we must have been eating it for some time, worms and all. My companions were all very frugal. When I could no longer get a spoon of oatmeal down and started limiting myself to bread, jam, and bologna, they all complained that my new meal plan cost too much. I was all for saving as much money as we could, but I had had enough of the oatmeal-and-worm casserole to last a lifetime! We calculated how much I had earned by how many rows I thinned, and I took my pay and left.

They figured I would be back, but I had other plans. After walking a few miles, I found a job making summer fallow. When that was done, I found another job driving a buck rake to make hay. The buck rake had one horse at each end, twelve feet apart, with one line for control of each horse. Unfortunately, although one of the horses was eager to work, the other was just plain lazy. After working hard to keep the lazy one on the job all day, I had had enough of him. After work, I jumped on that lazy horse, kicked him in the ribs, and made him buck with the harness on. Then I used a short whip and showed him who was boss. That horse must have spent the whole night rethinking his life, because the next day when I said, "Giddyup," he got right to work like the other horse and didn't give me any more trouble.

As each job was finished, I would find another, right through to the end of the summer. Once or twice I went to visit my companions on the beet farm, and when they were ready to go home to the McMahon area they came to get me. They figured they could save a few dollars if I came along to share the travel expenses, but I preferred to stay a bit longer in Alberta, having not yet forgotten the oatmeal episode. I was not ready to be connected to the "frugal oatmeal-eating bachelors" again! After working another job or two, I returned home just before harvest on the farm.

The profit I had made from making saddles and trading furs had started me thinking about possible new business ventures. Around that time, my older brother Peter and I started a shoe repair shop in the east side of our large barn. My father had bought a Singer sewing machine that could sew leather, and we began installing new soles and patching shoes. Eventually, Father told us it was getting too busy on the farm, with too much traffic and too many customers needing their shoes repaired. So we decided to focus on another project.

My father had bought an old thrashing machine (thresher), a Minneapolis Moline, for less than $100, but it needed to be rebuilt. Peter and I repaired the bearings by melting babbitt (bearing metal), pouring new molds, fitting the larger bearings, and rebuilding the wooden straw shakers. We were able to get the thrashing machine ready in time for harvest, but there was only a light crop that year.

In 1941 my two older brothers and I decided to offer our thrashing service using a 15–30 McCormick tractor on steel wheels. Winter came early that year, so we were not able to do much work, but in the early spring we were ready for business again. Farmers in the area had not had enough time in the fall to thrash, due to early snow, so there was plenty to do. We moved from farm to farm, with only our horses for transportation. Those horses were always good and tired by the end of the day—and so were we.

At one farm, I recall, we had to sleep in an empty granary that was not airtight. As a result, the temperature dropped below freezing during the nights we were there. When my ears began to freeze because we didn't have enough blankets, I wrapped my jacket around my ears. Unfortunately, I still woke up with a bad earache on the first morning, and when I woke up on the second morning the left side of my face was paralyzed! I couldn't close my eye, and to eat I had to hold out my cheek so I wouldn't bite into it. Boy, was I happy when we finished at that farm and went home!

I was seventeen that year and still full of energy and ideas, but the paralysis would not heal. For three months I had to try to stay out of the sun to protect my eye that was stuck open. What a sight I must have been! I passed the time building saddles and helping my mother, especially in the summer kitchen, and due to my condition, I became increasingly introverted and self-conscious. I didn't want to see anyone; nor did I want anyone to see me.

The war years had now begun in earnest. Peter had gone to work in an aircraft manufacturing factory in Fort William, Ontario. It had already been six months since my paralysis started and I was only slowly beginning to recover. There seemed to be no cure for the strange condition.

I recall asking my mother what would happen to me. Her response was simple and wise: "We need to pray." And pray she did. One day soon afterwards, I sensed a bit of feeling returning to my face, and I realized that it was an answer to my mother's prayer.

Life began to return to normal that fall. In my younger years I had started to pray to God when I attended Sunday school. Unfortunately, I soon found that I enjoyed fighting more than praying, and I stopped trying to pray. God had now showed me, though, that when my mother prayed, He heard her. This started me thinking but did not have an immediate major impact on my life. I was too busy with all of the activities of youth.

Three of my brothers and I especially enjoyed playing fastball. George was the best pitcher in southwest Saskatchewan, John was a good catcher, and Peter was good on first base. I, the youngest, was the third baseman. We played ball and practiced nearly every day. We got so good at the game that for a number of years all the schools in the area complained about how badly they got beat by the Rempel team. Father was unhappy with our devotion to fastball, since he viewed it as a waste of time, but time was something we had plenty of in those days.

In our teenage years, we would travel to all-day tournaments using the Model T. One such tournament was particularly memorable, because it was tougher than usual. The tournament was held at Lac Pelletier, twenty-five miles to the southwest. A professional baseball team thought they would put us in our place, but they couldn't hit the fast curve balls, and we won as usual.

Toward evening came the "winners' match," the Rempels against the other best team. The pitchers on both teams were very good, and halfway through the game no one had yet scored any runs. Finally, we got two men on base from a base hit and a walk.

It was my turn to bat, and I had had a lot of practice trying to hit George's challenging pitching. Being the competitor that I was, I always practiced hitting home runs. To my pleasant surprise, the first pitch was a beautiful throw right down the middle. Crack! I hit the ball just right, and it sailed over the pitcher, the second baseman, and center fielder. It took a long time to even find the ball!

In the end, we won the game and the prize of fifty dollars, which represented a month's wages for four. All nine players shared the winnings. Maybe Father wouldn't think this game was such a waste of time after all! Later, our team came to be called the Rhineland Rockets and became the best promotion for our village—spreading far and wide the name of the village that my father and grandfather had started thirty-five years earlier.

Rhineland Rocket ball team, 1943

CHAPTER IV

Helen

A wife of noble character who can find? She is worth far more than rubies. Her husband has full confidence in her and lacks nothing of value. She brings him good, not harm, all the days of her life. She selects wool and flax and works with eager hands. She is like the merchant ships, bringing her food from afar. She gets up while it is still dark; she provides food for her family and portions for her servant girls. She considers a field and buys it; out of her earnings she plants a vineyard. She sets about her work vigorously; her arms are strong for her tasks. She sees that her trading is profitable, and her lamp does not go out at night (Proverbs 31:10–18).

When I first met Helen, I quickly recognized that I had found a pearl of great price, rare and very valuable, with a bright, healthy mind and a very friendly personality. Later I realized it had been love at first sight.

It was a Sunday evening in late September or early October of 1942, just before I turned eighteen. A neighbor friend was able to borrow his family's new sedan and took me along for a ride. I told him that there was a young lady I had wanted to meet for some time, named Helen Wieler, and my friend agreed to make the trip to the Wieler farm, four miles from our village.

Frank's first suit, 1942

When we arrived, I went to the door and met with Mr. Henry Wieler, Helen's father. "Is Helen at home, and may I see her?" I asked. When Mr. Wieler agreed, Helen came out, and I introduced myself. When I saw her, I realized how young she was, but I still asked if she would like a ride in a nice car, and she said that she would. With her being so young, we didn't drive very far, but the ride was long enough for us get acquainted—and to have our first kiss! She was fourteen years old, and I was seventeen.

I quickly discovered that she was not only a beautiful girl with lovely eyes but also had a quick mind and an adventurous spirit. Unlike many in those days, she was quite eager to try new things and did not feel the need for her home to be her entire world. Since Helen was so young, though, I waited a year before going back for another visit.

Unfortunately, this time her father told me, "No way!" Helen really wanted to see me again, but because I wasn't a Christian her father rightly wouldn't let her. However, Helen's mother liked me and convinced him to let us see each other.

The Wieler family with Helen front right, 1942

Helen's father had been born in a Mennonite village near the city of Orenberg, in the Ural Mountain area of Eastern Russia. His mother died when he was only seven years old, and at that point he was taken in by the Harder family. In his teenage years, Henry became a Christian at some special meetings that were held in the area, but the Harder family did not approve of his "new religion," as they called it. Some time later, Henry had to serve in the army and was assigned to the medical corps. He served on the Crimean Peninsula when Russia was at war with Turkey, working long, hard hours to help wounded and dying soldiers. He recalled that he was once so tired he fell asleep in a bed with a man who had just died!

In 1918, at the end of the war, Henry was discharged. The army had just gotten in a big shipment of white sheets, and, not knowing what to do with them, they told the discharged soldiers that they could take whatever they wanted. So Henry stuffed a set of sheets in his suitcase and went home to Orenberg. When he married Agneta Wiebe in 1919, the white sheets became a beautiful wedding dress.

Soon, there was a famine, and the Wieler family had to struggle to find enough to eat. Even rodents became fair game. There were days when there was no food at all; and yet, by 1926, Henry and Agneta had five children. That year, a generous relative made it possible for them to migrate to Canada, right before the doors for emigration were closed by the Bolshevik government. The family had many close calls, both as they traveled across Russia and as they left the country, but in 1927 they finally arrived in Arcola, Saskatchewan, with several other families. There they rented a farm with some of their relatives, and on April 19, 1928, Helen came along.

Soon after, the family moved to Herbert, Saskatchewan, and a few years later they were able to settle on a small farm half a mile west of McMahon, Saskatchewan. Initially, their house consisted of just two rooms for Henry, Agneta, and the nine children they now had, and they had a barn made of straw and wire mesh.

Helen enjoyed her younger years. The Wieler family attended the Mennonite Brethren Church in Rhinefeld, several miles north of McMahon, and at age twelve Helen decided to become a follower of Jesus. She had been raised in a Christian family, but her parents were sour toward Christianity, even though they continued going to church. Helen swore she wouldn't become a Christian because her parents were so sour, and she wanted to be happy. But one night when she went to church, missionaries were speaking. The message was so compelling that when they gave an invitation for those who wanted to become followers of Jesus, Helen went forward and gave her life to the Lord. When she went home and told her parents that she had become a Christian, their response was "That's good; maybe you'll be a good girl now!"

Helen's father had bought an old pump organ for four dollars, and Helen taught herself to play. She enjoyed playing the organ at church and attending Sunday school. She also played fastball in school, which was the only sport they had there. Helen loved to be outside with her dad, but there was always so much work to do—especially weeding. They needed to try to plant and grow enough potatoes to get them through the winter. "I enjoyed living, but working those potatoes was not living!" Helen recalls.

When I met Helen in 1942, I knew that she was the girl for me, but I also knew that she was only fourteen years old. So, unfortunately, I had some waiting to do.

CHAPTER V

Farmhand, Cowboy, and Hobo

To get my foot into the stirrup I needed to stand on either a rock or a water trough. The fact was that I was still quite small in stature, and the more I had to struggle to get on a horse, the more I wanted to ride. It was much faster and easier than walking, and less tiring than running. During trapping season, in particular, the horse could travel better through the snow.

Bronc riding was an exciting adventure beginning in my early teen years. One of my earliest experiences came in 1940 when a brother-in-law wanted me to ride one of his "team horses," as he called it. "I have no saddle," he said. And so I had to do the job bareback.

Unfortunately, the horse was a razorback, with a sharp backbone sticking out. When the horse crowhopped and bucked quite vigorously, I soon found myself in severe pain. When I finished the ride the pain only got worse. I found from experience that a broken tailbone is not only extremely painful but is also very slow to heal, especially if you keep on riding after the damage has been done. After that, I was always sure to use a saddle to ride broncs!

The following year, a neighbor asked me to break his very frisky four-year-old horse. I asked, "Where do you want me to ride him?"

He told me, "I have a large front yard that should work." The horse was halter broke, and I thought it would be safer not to use a bridle and bit, but only having the halter made it impossible to control the direction of the horse. When the horse began to buck very hard and found that he couldn't throw me, he tried to rub me off against the buildings. This was one smart horse! Then he thought he would try taking me under a clothesline. When it didn't work the first time, he whirled around and went under again.

Finally, the horse played himself out. I made him walk for a while and then dismounted and put a bridle and bit on him. I thought he had learned who was boss, but as I went to climb back on, that horse reared his head back and smacked me in the face, leaving me with a severe black eye!

On many farms and ranches in those days, you could find a horse that was "too wild to ride." Two years later, in 1943, I was at a farm in southern Alberta to help make summer fallow (tilling the land to control weeds in years the farmers left the land idle). Sure enough, the boss pointed to a horse and told me that whatever I did, "Don't ride him!" Well, one day when the boss was gone, a few of us had too much time on our hands after supper. I was ready for a challenge. When I was young, no matter how long the workday was, I always seemed to have energy to spare.

The bronco that "couldn't be rode," 1943

We put our heads together and decided how we would handle the wild one. He was all right with a halter on him. Working from outside the stall, we were able to put a saddle on him. When we turned him loose, though, he bucked so hard that somehow the saddle and a sack of grain we had tied on it both came off. A horse that can buck a saddle all the way off might be hard to ride! My solution was to tell the others, "He's too dangerous to ride with the saddle. I'll ride him bareback!"

To try to take some of the fight out of him we blindfolded him. As I came close and touched him, he started kicking, but I wasn't ready to give up. We put a long rope on the halter, and with one man controlling the rope and the horse blindfolded, I took a running jump and landed on his back.

That horse was bucking before I could remove the blindfold. He was going toward a fence, but my helper yanked on the rope. The horse fell, but I was able to jump clear and then get back on before he was up all the way. When the blindfold finally came off, that horse saw me on top of him and threw himself down hard. This time, I didn't have a chance to jump. That ornery horse rolled on top of me, right up to my shoulders, and then rolled back the other way for good measure. When he stood up, his front hoof was right in front of my face.

I was thankful that the horse stood perfectly still while I crawled out slowly from underneath. My face was bruised from hitting the ground. That night, for the first time that I could remember, I couldn't sleep because of a question going through my mind: "What if?" That could have been my last ride. If it had, where would I be now?

A Sunday school teacher had made it clear to me, as a twelve-year-old, that heaven and hell are real places. As I thought about my close brush with death, I realized I wouldn't have made it to heaven, and I was afraid, more afraid than I had ever been before in my life. But my fears didn't stop me from breaking that horse so that he could be ridden without bucking. In time, I rode him to a standstill with a bridle in a soft summer fallow field.

Conquering that horse took away my fears, but the lingering memory of what that wild horse had done to me and how close I had come to the end has never left me right to this day. I learned a valuable lesson about avoiding unnecessary risks when riding broncs, and I began asking questions that would be important later.

Some time after that incident, I caught a freight train to Calgary with another cowboy. I was going to ride broncs in the Calgary Stampede, but

I found the entry fee too high. I might lose money if I didn't do well in the competition, I thought. That night, though, I went to a barn dance and danced with a cowgirl. When I walked her back to her tent, she asked, "You wanna stay?"

My mother's careful training paid off, and I had the good sense to say, "Thanks, but I shouldn't do that. I can't stay with you." I was tempted, but I kissed her goodnight and walked away.

My traveling partner and I were staying in a hostel at the time. It was twenty-five cents a night, with two to a bed and six beds to a room. When the bedbugs made us leave after two nights of constant scratching, we decided to catch the night train south to Lethbridge. It was a hair-raising experience, catching a train at night. We had to run alongside the train on a sloping gravel shoulder and then grab the ladder at the rear of the boxcar. It was very important to make sure that you got first one foot and then the other one on the rung of the ladder very quickly. Otherwise, the momentum would carry you around the corner of the car, and you would lose your hold and end up under the wheels of the next car. (I know this because it almost happened to me one time when the train we were catching was picking up speed too fast. Thankfully, my traveling partner had gone on first and was able to help me regain my footing.)

It was very cold, and we ran along the top of the cars to get to the coal car, where there were warm pipes for some comfort. We arrived at Lethbridge at dawn. After the train had crossed a trestle traveling very slowly, we jumped off and went beneath the bridge. We took off our clothes, had a bath in the river, and washed all of our clothes. The bedbugs were finally gone, but the itch remained! Since there was no one there who would listen anyway, we decided not to complain.

From the river, we walked into town and bought a pound of wieners and a loaf of bread. We decided to try to get back to a farm south of Grassy Lake, where we knew the farmers still needed help to get ready for harvest. We knew that we would also likely be needed for more plowing of the summer fallow weeds. My plans, though, quickly changed. I had written home to tell my family where I was, and I now received a letter from my mother saying that she would like me to come home to help them with harvest. So I traveled home just before harvest.

One of the challenging parts of being a hobo is finding a place to stay at night. In summertime, empty boxcars made the best sleeping quarters. We would keep the door of the car open a few inches by jamming in a piece of wood, which usually could be found in one of the cars. That way the door would not lock us in. When the train started off again, the jolt could easily open or close an unjammed door. We figured if someone else tried to enter, we would hear the noise of the door opening. "Homosexuals are dangerous," my traveling partner said. "We have to be prepared to jump awake and be ready to fight at any time." This habit of jumping out of my sleep almost got me into trouble years later when I got married and Helen would move or say something while I was sleeping.

Life is like a mountain railroad, with an engineer that's brave;
We must make the run successful, from the cradle to the grave.
Watch the curves, the fills, the tunnels;
never falter, never quail.
Keep your hand upon the throttle,
and your eye upon the rail.

Blessed Savior, Thou wilt guide us,
till we reach that blissful shore.
Where the angels wait to join us
in Thy praise forevermore.
("Life Is like A Mountain Railroad"
—M. E. Abbey and Charles Davis Tillman, 1890)

The warm summer day had a pleasant air. I sat on an isolated step of a caboose car in southern Alberta, waiting for the train to begin moving. The conductor saw me, just as the train started. He shouted, "Where do you think you're going, young man?"

I said, "I'm on my way to Medicine Hat, where this train's headed."

"Well, get off!" he responded. "You're not catching a ride on my train!"

I dutifully got off, then let the caboose go by before running to the other side and catching the ladder of the last boxcar. Unfortunately, the conductor was just as smart as I was, and he spotted me again. He crawled up on top of the car, looked down, shook his fist at me, and told me to jump. The train was picking up speed, and I realized that I could resist or jump. I chose to jump and landed hard but stayed on my feet, running downhill into a ditch. My high-heeled cowboy boots were definitely a liability in this type of activity!

I soon was limping along in pain. I was not inclined to walk any distance at that point, so I waited patiently beside a grain elevator for the next train to come along. I was able to catch this train while it was still moving slowly, and I arrived in Medicine Hat at about sunset. It was early fall of 1943, and I was on my way home to Swift Current after spending the summer working for wages, bronc riding, and being a hobo.

The troop train, Medicine Hat, Alberta, 1943

In Medicine Hat that night, I thought it was time to buy a bus ticket home. The bus depot was in the train station, and the next bus didn't leave until after midnight. So I held off buying a ticket, just in case I might catch a ride somehow.

I went to sleep on a bench, and after about three hours I woke up and saw a lot of people standing on the dock outside. I asked, "What's up?" and was told there was a troop train coming in that would make a brief stop. Soon the train came into view, with its two steam engines coming to a stop a short distance past the station. I walked through a poorly lit area and stood a little ahead of the engines. I noticed that the military police were standing guard.

When the engine started moving, I sprinted to the coal car behind the engine. It was only a short distance, but the engines picked up speed much faster than I had thought possible. Then I heard a military policeman holler at me, "Stop!" I was smart enough to realize I had better hide quickly. I made it up the ladder and between the cars, out of sight.

My initial fears subsided as I crawled up a ladder and sat on top of the coal car, where there was some shelter from the wind. I was sitting very close behind the engine.

The train went nonstop to Swift Current, taking about two hours. Fortunately it slowed down enough so that I could jump off again, landing at a run. I then slowly walked to a restaurant on Railway Street. The washroom was in the basement, and finding the mirror I realized how fortunate I was to be alone. I was covered with black coal dust and soot. To my advantage, my cowboy hat, shirt, jacket, pants, and boots had already been black, as black clothes were my regular cowboy uniform. I was alone in the washroom as I shook out my clothes and used a wet towel to clean them. My face was another matter. It took several rounds with a bar of soap before I could begin to find my skin underneath all that soot and coal dust! When I was done I found a place in a basement storage room and dozed off until morning.

When I took another look in the mirror the next morning, I realized I would have to spend fifty cents for a shave and haircut. "What happened to you?" asked the barber.

"I had to shovel coal," I told him. Cleaned up a bit, I found a ride to a village close to home. It cost me two bits for the twenty-five miles to the village. From there I walked the last two miles home, stored away my cowboy hat, jacket, and boots, changed into farm clothing, and said hello to my mother.

She asked if I had had a hard time away from home all summer. I told her I had worked very hard and saved my money so that I could help her and Dad pay the bills. No need to tell her about the "adventure" parts!

Life back on the farm seemed restful compared to the summer away, and I was ready to settle in to life at home for the few months of fall, helping to store feed from a meager dried-out crop.

CHAPTER VI

A New Life

I n the midst of my busy life and adventures, I had not forgotten Helen. It was now almost two years since I had taken her for a ride. I had spent the summer of 1944 working a job on a farm in Alberta, and while I was there I had written a letter to Helen. When I returned home after the summer, I went to see her. I quickly discovered that the Friday evening "young people service" at a church in McMahon was a good place to meet with her.

Helen's family had moved two miles south of McMahon, and she and her sister Laura would ride their horses to the meetings. After the meetings, we would all lead our horses and walk home to their farm together. Laura would walk ahead of us so that we could have time to enjoy each other's company privately. Helen, who was now sixteen years old, had always wanted to be a cowgirl, so she really liked this cowboy coming to see her, riding his horse and wearing a black hat. "Those were very exciting times," she recalled, "and the letter that I received helped me to decide who I wanted to come see me."

Around the time of Helen's seventeenth birthday in 1945, I started looking for a ring—just in case! I saw a diamond ring at a jewelers, but the diamond was too small for my taste. My pearl of great price needed something bigger! A year earlier I had started a garage business, which was bringing me more steady income. So when I found a ring with a larger diamond I was able to buy it right away.

Helen, 1946

I went to see Helen. "I know you're too young, but will you marry me?" I asked.

Helen said yes. Helen's Aunt Tina was there at the time, and she asked her, "Are you sure you want to do this? You're awfully young." Helen insisted that she was sure.

Having made that commitment, we began making plans to marry a year later. I bought four acres of land and built a two-room home (fourteen feet by twenty-eight feet). In those days, the norm was for young couples to get married and move in with their parents until they could get a place of their own, but I was never one to stand on tradition, and I was determined to have a place of our own on our wedding day.

Finally, the big day arrived. On Sunday, August 25, 1946, Helen and I were married. It had rained very heavily the night before, and the roads were muddy. Helen's parents graciously invited my parents to their house for a lunch of borsch and other tasty dishes. My dad especially loved it!

Our wedding day, 1946

Early that afternoon we traveled to the church and found it nearly full of friends and relatives waiting to witness our marriage. I remember being very nervous. I didn't like being the center of attention at all. But Helen's calmness helped me tremendously, and her stunning beauty distracted me from my anxiety.

After the wedding, we traveled the ten miles from Rhinefeld to Rhineland and spent our honeymoon in the cabin I had built. Although it was our own place, the two-room house was also a pioneer home. The water system was a galvanized barrel in the house. I had to haul the water to fill the barrel, since we didn't have a well. We had an outhouse and no electricity. We were able to buy a wood cookstove to heat the house and the water for cooking, washing, etc., but with the long war just ending it was almost impossible to buy other basic necessities. Even finding material to buy clothes was out of the question. We didn't have much at all in those days, but we had each other; and our love for one another easily made up for the things we lacked.

When Christmas came, we found that Helen was carrying our first child, and on June 12, 1947, Stanley James Rempel was born. The feeling of responsibility that came with Stan's birth was more than I expected, and I was afraid that I was not ready to give my son the kind of direction and spiritual leadership he would need. I knew I had much to learn about being a father.

The summer months that year were very busy, but Helen and I both became restless. For me, it was my independent spirit. Shortly before we had gotten married, my brother Peter had joined me in the garage business, and we had added a store soon after. The partnership with my wife, Helen, was for life, but the business partnership was no longer satisfying our needs; nor was it what we wanted as a lifestyle for Helen and me. Our world needed to be bigger, and Helen was willing to try something new.

We made plans together, and then one day I approached my brother Peter. "You can have the store and the garage business," I told him, "and I'll take the half-tonne truck [which was paid for]." Peter was happy, and Helen and I were now free to sell our little house, load up our few belongings, and move to Clearbrook, British Columbia, in October of 1947.

Stan was just four months old when we set out on this new adventure, looking for a new life together. I began searching for work immediately to support my young family and soon found a job as a cleanup person on the night shift at a business called Stave Lake Cedar, north of Mission, BC, on the Dewdney Trunk Road. The company sawed cedar shingles and shakes.

This was a time of major changes in my life, and the shock of being away from family and giving up the security that our business had provided suddenly brought uncertainties and questions to my life. Feeling the added responsibilities of supporting a family led me to begin searching for an anchor for my life and for peace within for both the present and for the future.

This sense of need only intensified when I had a near-fatal accident. I was coming home from my nightshift at 4:00 a.m., driving from Mission to Clearbrook, when I came to Highway 1, where I would stop and turn right. Suddenly I had no brakes, and the car went across the highway before I could get the emergency brake on. I somehow missed all the cross traffic. The next day the brakes worked just fine, and they never failed again. What in the world had happened?

I remembered that when my mother had prayed for me, my paralysis had begun to heal. And I wondered if God might listen if I prayed to Him myself. I had this inner fear that I was not meant to be a Christian. I felt that quite likely God didn't want me, but I started to pray nevertheless. I would pray during my midnight break and at my lunch break. I told the Lord, "Lord, if you could let me be a Christian, I might be willing to go to church."

Several incidents, though, like making a poor decision regarding what vehicle to buy, only increased my insecurity. After some days of struggling with anxiety on my own, I began to pray again. I had heard many years before that we are all sinners, separated from God because of our sins. I knew that God had sent His Son Jesus to die in my place and that He required that I choose to turn from my sins and embrace Jesus as my Lord and Savior.

One night on my lunch break in my car I prayed, "Lord, I believe You are real. I'm going to put my total trust in You because I have nowhere else to go." I didn't trust pastors and certainly wasn't willing to talk to any pastor I knew. Growing up, it was only on rare occasions that my family would attend church together. All of the boys would sit in the back benches on the right and the men in the front. On the other side, the girls sat in the back and the women in the front. The singing involved chanting songs without any music. None of us understood much from the sermons, except for the constant warnings to obey, though we weren't ever told who we were supposed to obey or why. When I got older and I was supposed to go through catechism classes and then be baptized, I told my parents that I would not be participating. This was particularly hard on my mother, since all of my siblings were much more compliant than I was.

Now as a husband and father myself, I didn't have a church to turn to for help and hadn't discussed my trials or stress with anyone. That night, though, as I was praying, a presence came into the car with me. The presence surrounded me, like a cloak or a warm blanket wrapping around me. A great peace flooded my heart. With it came great joy and deep emotion. I don't remember ever crying before that time, but suddenly I had tears running down my face. In a very brief time, my uncertainties all went away. I went back to work, finished my shift, and drove home at 4:30 a.m.

As soon as I got home, I woke Helen up and tried to tell her that something happened. I told her that I had prayed and I believed that I had become a Christian. I had been a bit afraid to tell her, because neither of us thought highly about church, but she immediately told me that she had prayed a similar prayer a week earlier to rededicate her life to the Lord. I had always respected her lifestyle, but she had never said anything about being a Christian. It was November 7, 1947, and I was twenty-three years old.

On the night shift at work, there were eight or nine Asian workers—Japanese and Chinese. Some of them smoked pot, which made them smell bad. I didn't like these Asians. They were dirty, and I kept away from them. But the next night, having given my life to the Lord, somehow they looked nicer to me and I became friendly toward them. My life had changed overnight, and I began a friendship where before I had just avoided them. In time they began to show interest in me too, and we became friends and enjoyed working together.

With our new life in Christ, what wonderful love, joy, and peace came into our household! We both knew that we were new creations through what Jesus Christ had done for us through His death and resurrection. He had taken away our sins, made us new people, and given us the gift of eternal life. Suddenly, all of the uncertainties were gone; my search for an anchor for my life was over. Now I was a follower of Jesus Christ; He would chart the course of my life. As God's child, I could be assured that He would take care of me as a loving Heavenly Father, both now and when I died. With our new life and new hearts we had a wonderful winter living in Clearbrook, BC.

CHAPTER VII

Learning to Trust and to Give

It was 1948, and I was still with Stave Lake Cedar but now was working as a shingle sawyer (a person who saws shingles). My job was financially rewarding, but it was also very risky. It was quite easy to lose a finger, or even a limb, in this line of work. But the Lord graciously kept me safe. I thoroughly enjoyed what I was doing, and I was making many friends at work.

During the first week of April, we received word that my father was very ill. I was told that if I wanted to see him I would have to hurry home to Rhineland. So we set out by train, but we were met by severe winter weather and huge snowdrifts along the way. It was a challenging trip, and I was grateful that we were able to make it to Rhineland in time to see my dad. I told him that I had become a Christian and asked him if I would see him in heaven. He said, "Yes, and when I see Jesus I will ask Him why it had to be so hard and heavy here on earth." Those were his last words before he went into a coma. My father passed away on the first day of spring weather, April 14, 1948, at the age of sixty-two.

That same year, the Fraser Valley experienced one of the greatest floods to ever strike that part of BC. Although the floodwaters didn't affect our house, Stave Lake Cedar was flooded out, and there was no telling when I would have work again. So Helen and I decided to move to southern Alberta, where two of Helen's sisters and their husbands had recently moved to work as farm laborers. My new job was to help develop land for irrigation. We were desperately poor and had left our car in BC to be sold, along with many of our belongings, but we had found new life in Jesus Christ. We moved to a farm south of Purple Springs and discovered a country church nearby—Mennonite Brethren. After some time, we decided to be baptized and join the church.

Stanley at Purple Springs, 1952

At first, Helen's relatives could not understand why we would want to be baptized, and they criticized us. Then one of Helen's sisters went through renewal in her own life and decided to join the church with us. Her husband also professed to becoming a believer and decided to join us in baptism. Then, two days before our baptism, the other brother-in-law went to see a pastor and also became a follower of Jesus. So in the end, five of us were baptized together in the Old Man River on a cold, rainy Sunday afternoon in June, and six new members were added to the little Mennonite Brethren church. I was still twenty-three years old.

Our baptism was followed by our first communion service. It was a very emotional time for both of us, with lots of hugging and kissing with our new "brethren" as we were welcomed as new members of the church.

The Grassy Lake Church elders said it was their greatest revival, with their attendance increasing by about 20 percent! We attended faithfully, even though joining in the Bible reading and prayer in the services in the German language was hard.

Baptized in Old Man River north of Purple Springs, 1949

Am I a soldier of the cross,
A follower of the Lamb,
And shall I fear to own His cause
Or blush to speak His name?

Must I be carried to the skies
On flowery beds of ease,
While others fought to win the prize,
And sailed through bloody seas?

Are there no foes for me to face?
Must I not stem the flood?
Is this vile world a friend to grace,
To help me on to God?
Sure I must fight, if I would reign;
Increase my courage, Lord.
I'll bear the toil, endure the pain,
Supported by Thy word.

Thy saints in all this glorious war
Shall conquer, though they die;
They see the triumph from afar,
By faith's discerning eye.

When that illustrious day shall rise,
And all Thy armies shine
In robes of victory through the skies,
The glory shall be Thine.

("Am I a Soldier of the Cross?"—Isaac Watts, 1721)

One day, a missionary came to speak at the church. He was on leave after serving four years in Ethiopia and spoke with great passion about the need to spread the gospel to all nations. This, in fact, is the central commission that God has given to His people. We are to be His ambassadors in this world. On that day, Helen and I recognized that although we were not equipped to go as missionaries, we could certainly send others. We realized that God had given us the gift of giving financially. And so, from our very meager income, we began to tithe. We learned how to live on 90 percent of what we made. Later, we increased our giving to a larger proportion of our income.

Early in our time in the Purple Springs area, one of my older brothers, a neighbor, and I bought most of a business together: McMahon Motors. As a result, we moved back to McMahon, Saskatchewan. The company sold wood, gas, oil, and hardware and was a Cockshutt farm machinery dealership. We quickly added groceries and a Chevrolet agency. But, after two crop failures in the area and a partnership that went very sour, we soon found ourselves broke again. The neighbor we had gone into business with held more shares in the business than either myself or my brother and decided to sell some of his shares to a relative. The two of them then had the controlling shares of the business and decided to sell it without our approval.

My brother decided to take what he could from the business and leave. I, on the other hand, told the shareholders that I would take the grocery inventory in exchange for my shares, and they agreed. But when the sale was about to go through, the buyer insisted that the grocery inventory be included in the deal. When the shareholders told me I could not have the groceries, I told them that I would take them anyway. They warned me, though, that since our agreement was not in writing they would call the police if I tried to take what was mine. In the end, like my father after the colony land swindle, we were left with nothing. Our second partnership in a business had been a painful failure.

Helen and I moved back to a farm south of Purple Springs, Alberta. It took us three years to work through the terrible memories and feelings of loss from our experience in McMahon. The hardest thing to deal with was the shock that our Christian partner had not kept his word. As a result of his dishonest business dealings, we lost all of our assets. But not all was bleak during those years. On February 23, 1951, our second child, Stuart, was born in the Tabor, Alberta, hospital. We were now a family of four.

After three years in the Purple Springs area, we moved to Swift Current, Saskatchewan, in March of 1953, and it is still home for us in 2012! The fact that I had gained experience overhauling motors in my late teen years helped me get a job with Century Motors, a GM dealership, and in 1955 I became a journeyman mechanic.

Soon after moving to Swift Current, Helen and I met a young missionary couple, Pastor Lawrence Redekop and his wife, who had been sent to begin a Sunday school for all ages on the south side of Swift Current. They had started the Southside Mission church plant, and Helen was chosen as their first Sunday school teacher. I helped gather the children on Sunday mornings and also became a teacher as the Sunday morning service grew larger. We rebuilt an old air-base building for our meetings but soon outgrew that building and had to move into the city.

Around January 1956, I developed some serious health problems as a result of carbon monoxide poisoning. I had been working in an enclosed stall and had not noticed that the fan that ventilated it had quit working. Soon the stall filled with carbon monoxide, and I collapsed. I was able to crawl out of the stall, but the damage had been done; I was simply too ill to work after that, and my journeyman mechanic days were over.

The university hospital had no cure for the damage done by the carbon monoxide, and I was left with no income and no workmen's compensation. That winter was very long. We now had three children, with our beautiful daughter Connie Ruth having joined Stan and Stuart on August 17, 1955.

My health problems were the latest setback for us, but we pressed on and learned important lessons. Because of tragedy and defeat we began to fast and pray at intervals. The new church plant, Southside Mission, continued to grow, and Helen and I, with our children in tow, took part in the teaching. When early spring came, I began to pray and fast and look to the Lord for a way to pay our bills.

We were living in a two-room cabin again, which I had built a few years before. Earnestly seeking God's answer for us, we read a letter sent to us by Theodore Epp, from Back to the Bible, and he mentioned something called "adventuring by faith." He said that as a young man he had owned a business but felt the Lord leading him to start a broadcasting ministry. He needed money to get into this ministry and didn't have any. He decided to "adventure by faith" and wrote a check to pay for a radio tower, even though he didn't have the money. He then prayed and watched as the Lord supplied the funds to cover the check.

Helen and I decided to step out in faith ourselves, and we applied to the city for a lot that might be designated for a business and a store. We didn't have any money, but we fasted, prayed, and trusted the Lord to do His work. At first the city was against having a business in that location, but after much consideration they decided the corner lot did fit into their business plans. What an answer to our prayers and fasting!

Following Theodore Epp's example, we had given a check to the city to purchase the lot, but they didn't know that we did not yet have the money in our account to cover the check! Although the bank expected the sale to go through quickly, as we fasted and prayed for an answer the sale was delayed. Several weeks went by, and we finally decided to put our 1952 half-tonne Chevy truck up for sale. It wasn't long before a farmer and his son came and bought the truck for cash.

You can guess what we did with the money. We immediately deposited it into our bank account, and within two days the sale of the property went through. Our check to the city cleared, and we were the proud owners of a corner lot in Swift Current. We had paid $550 for it.

CHAPTER VIII

From Journeyman to Businessman

Do you not know? Have you not heard? The Lord *is the everlasting God, the Creator of the ends of the earth. He will not grow tired or weary, and his understanding no one can fathom. He gives strength to the weary and increases the power of the weak. Even youths grow tired and weary, and young men stumble and fall; but those who hope in the* Lord *will renew their strength. They will soar on wings like eagles; they will run and not grow weary, they will walk and not be faint* (Isaiah 40:28–31).

It was March 1956, and springtime would soon arrive. But I had no energy at all, and my health was a disaster. Thanks to the carbon monoxide, I had lost all of my teeth at the age of thirty-two. I had no appetite at all and was living on a diet of carrot juice, and I had boils. The greatest discomfort, though, was having no job and no income. What I did have was three children and a beautiful healthy wife. These were my assets. We also had the corner lot in Swift Current. God had answered our prayers and fasting, and we had a plan for the future but lacked a source of immediate income.

One day a neighbor came to see me. He was looking for someone to sell cookware. I was a journeyman motor mechanic with poor health, no teeth, and no other plans. But how does one make the switch from being a journeyman mechanic to a Renaware Cookware salesman?

The answer was not to be found simply in my own efforts. I realized that "Man does not live on bread alone, but on every word that comes from the mouth of God" (Matthew 4:4). I believed God, and I believed His promises, and my trust in Him freed up all sorts of creative energy in me. Trusting God to take care of us allowed me to take one day at a time.

By faith—a small faith perhaps, but faith in a Great God—Helen and I focused our attention not on seeking personal gain, but rather on fulfilling the purposes for which God had created us. And we found that just as He had created us, so had He given us the gift of being able to create new things as we followed His leading and used His strength. We, too, could make something out of nothing as we followed Him.

Four things shaped our approach to life at that time:

1. We committed ourselves to maintaining a positive attitude. We knew we couldn't grumble and trust God at the same time.
2. We committed ourselves to viewing the future as a challenge—and I loved challenges. We would not shy away from something just because it might bring more suffering. We knew by that time that great suffering often leads to great victory and blessing.
3. We recognized that God had given us a great commodity in the form of time, and we wanted to make the most of it.
4. We committed ourselves to seeking godly wisdom to use our strength and abilities to their fullest potential, so that we could glorify God with our lives.

Over the years, we have watched as God brought other people into our lives who had just the right resources at just the right time. As we tried to honor God one day at a time, we faced the question of how someone becomes a Renaware salesman without any money. It would take $35 for a down payment to purchase the sales kit, which included samples. Again we took our needs to the Lord in prayer.

One day on a street in Swift Current I saw a Syrian man whose vehicles I had repaired many times. He asked me what I was doing those days, and I told him I was trying to find a way to get $35 for the down payment on the sales kit. He immediately told me, "I don't have it with me, but I'll go and get it and bring it to you." His name was George, and I have never forgotten his kindness to me, but he wasn't the only one who helped me get started in my sales career.

You see, the sales kit was not the only thing I needed to get started. In rural Saskatchewan, a salesman also needed transportation, and I no longer owned a car, but I did have a good friend. His name was Ralph, and I had worked for him at the Century Motors GM dealership before the carbon monoxide poisoning. Ralph said to me one day, "I have this 1946 Pontiac that's in good shape. I'm planning to buy a new car, so I can sell you mine for a good price." Well, that was just the offer I needed!

The only problem was that I had no money. I told him, "Not only do I have no money, but I don't know when I will. I can't tell you when I will be able to pay you for the car."

Ralph responded, "I know you. You'll pay when you can; there's no hurry."

Just like that, I had my sales kit and a car to get around in. Once again God had provided for Helen and me, and we were learning to trust Him more and more for all of the practical details of our everyday lives.

Now, there were just two more challenges that I needed to overcome: I had to memorize my sales presentation, and I had to buy a set of teeth. It's difficult enough for a mechanic to learn to speak for a living; it's that much more difficult when that mechanic's only teeth is a set he purchased from a store! Every salesman needs a good smile, and mine certainly needed some work.

"Sacrifice thank offerings to God, fulfill your vows to the Most High, and call upon me in the day of trouble; I will deliver you, and you will honor me" (Psalm 50:14–15).

When someone finds himself without the proper resources, there's always an opportunity to learn to be humble. Humility can be described as a lack of arrogance; it's not weakness.

A humble person recognizes that he or she needs a support system. My primary support system has always been my wife Helen. She is encouraging, loyal, and a prayer warrior. In those days, when I was making a sales demonstration, I frequently sensed an unexpected and unseen Helper, and I seemed to always be able to finalize a sale.

Hiring and training other salesmen was part of my workday. With a salesman-in-training frequently along with me on my sales calls, I often heard them tell me that I was a poor salesman. The new guys, of course, firmly believed that they could do better, and I sincerely hoped they would. But I was the one who became a supervisor and won many sales prizes! The Lord seemed to give me favor with customers, and I knew that it was in answer to Helen's faithful prayers for me.

My profits became larger as the months went by, and Helen and I soon got to a point where we were living debt-free. That felt good! Our goal now was to find a way to provide a more suitable place for us and our three children to live.

Blessed is the man who finds wisdom, the man who gains understanding, for she is more profitable than silver and yields better returns than gold. She is more precious than rubies; nothing you desire can compare with her. Long life is in her right hand; in her left hand are riches and honor. Her ways are pleasant ways, and all her paths are peace. She is a tree of life to those who embrace her; those who lay hold of her will be blessed (Proverbs 3:13–18).

And so we began our building project on the corner lot. We designed the building with our dwelling on one story and space for our future store above us. This would become our home for the next eight years. When we had bought the lot, we told the city that we planned to build a store that we would call Hillcrest Shopping Centre. We hoped at the time to open it within the next couple of years. Four years had now passed since we left the Alberta farm job and settled in Swift Current. Our income had increased ten times over, and we increased our giving to God's work to match. We didn't know what the future held, but we knew who held the future in His hands.

The commercial corner lot that we had purchased was on the edge of the city, with nothing next to us but open prairie. One day, we heard an announcement that a huge CMHC-financed development was coming to Swift Current, right next to our property! The new development would be called the Hillcrest Area, named after our store, which had not yet opened. What an opportunity! Based on this information, Helen and I decided to open Hillcrest Shopping Centre as soon as possible.

"For God did not give us a spirit of timidity, but a spirit of power, of love and of self-discipline" (2 Timothy 1:7).

How, though, could we start a new store? We had already built a small building, with living quarters on one floor and a second floor ready for business, cookware sales, and hiring and training of personnel. But all of our assets were now tied up in the property and building, leaving no funds for actually starting the business. Although my work as a salesman was going well and allowed me to put my competitive spirit to good use, it also took me away from home and family far too much, and Helen and I were ready for a change.

It was time to open the store. We were coming to realize in those days that sometimes we tried too hard to go it alone and that was not the way to start a business or keep a business growing. I was starting to see just how valuable friendship can be. In fact, a network of friends would become our greatest asset in building our businesses. Of all the ships in the world, *friendship* truly has the longest life and takes us on the best voyage. It is also one of the most satisfying things in this life. A man or woman with many true friends is a wealthy person indeed.

This time my friendship with my former boss, Jack Carter, was the key means the Lord provided for starting the store business. Jack was a very positive influence on me and taught me many things. His help, once again, came at just the right time. I was learning how important credit is for building a business; and as we prayed for wisdom about opening the store, Helen and I decided to take out a loan from the bank. With our financial status, though, we would need someone to co-sign for the loan. Jack Carter graciously volunteered to sign for us.

What a blessing it was to have such a friend! But even as we were learning lessons about friendship, Helen and I were also increasingly realizing just how true the popular song was: "What a Friend We Have in Jesus"! More and more, we sought to honor Him one day at a time with our lives. We wanted to live by 1 Corinthians 10:31, which says, "So whether you eat or drink or whatever you do, do it all for the glory of God."

Our resources for the store were still very limited, but we built our own wooden shelves and decided to start small rather than wait. We had our grand opening in November 1957. The suppliers tried to make it a pre-Christmas bonanza, extending a line of credit to us that went far beyond what we expected. We had bought an adding machine, which Helen could operate with great efficiency. She, in fact, became the backbone of our store operation.

Hillcrest, the new store, 1957

In the spring of 1958, road construction for the new subdivision began, and all of a sudden the only way customers could get near our store was by walking. Needless to say, our business plummeted. At that point, Jack Carter came with a proposition: "Come and sell cars for me. That way, you'll be closer to home than selling cookware, and I know you can do it. I want you to sell my used cars."

I told him frankly, "I'm a mechanic, and I always know what's wrong with a car. I can't sell a car without letting people know whether or not it's in good working condition."

He said, "You'll find a way to make it work, and I'll pay you an extra generous rate of commission. No salary." Well, that sounded like a challenge to me. I guess Jack had learned by then how to motivate me!

There were three other professional salesmen working for him, and my competitive spirit kicked in immediately. Soon I had sold all the old used cars Jack Carter had sitting on his car lot. He came to me one day and asked in astonishment, "How have you done it? You haven't had even one bad deal so far, even though all used cars need attention." Once again, as I sought to honor God in all things, he was blessing me.

"For the LORD gives wisdom" (Proverbs 2:6).

I was committed to keeping my value system in order in all areas of life, but at that point I was especially focused on doing so when selling used cars. How could I justify selling a clunker to an unsuspecting customer? My solution was simple: I would openly tell them what I saw the car needed. Then, if they bought it, they would know that nothing had been hidden. It would be clear what they were buying. Once the customer heard this, he would ask me how much it would cost to fix, and I would introduce him to a serviceman or the foreman, who would tell him. Many customers asked for a discount, but I told them if they wanted a discount there would be no warranty. They could have one or the other. My conscience was clear, and my sales boomed!

Not everything about my new job, however, was rosy. My biggest struggle in those days was the criticism I faced from co-workers. As I seemed to close the deal with everyone I tried to sell a car to, the older salesmen started complaining that I was stealing their sales. I was just doing my job, and my competitive spirit wouldn't let me back down. In fact, as I think about it, I had rarely given an inch over the nearly thirty-four years I had been on the planet to that point!

Jack Carter decided I needed to take the Dale Carnegie course "How to Make Friends and Influence Others," and I was happy to comply. I ended up graduating as the impromptu speech champion, and after that I tried to disagree with my fellow salesmen in a more friendly way!

Meanwhile, Helen was busy running the store, and with me occupied selling used cars, she needed help. We were grateful to the Lord when our nephew came along to work part-time after school. Waldy was about thirteen years old when he stared working for us and continued working part-time at the store until he turned eighteen. At that point, he began working full-time in the summer months and attending university during the school year. In this way he worked his way through college, and to my knowledge he graduated with no debt. We hired other clerks over the years as well. One of them, Doris Bornn, would later become the new owner of the store.

Finally, the new subdivision became a reality. Business increased, and Helen carried the load of administrator, record keeper, and general supervisor. She also started a bakeshop, selling doughnuts, buns, and bread. Profits increased, and life was very busy and prosperous.

On January 25, 1960, our daughter Donna Jane was born. She was beautiful, healthy, and adorable. Jane spent much of her earliest days in a shopping cart that we made into a bed for her. We now had four children, two boys and two girls, and Helen continued to help around the store as well as caring for them.

CHAPTER IX

The Christian Service Brigade

Now we trust in God to keep us
bright and keen for Christ
because we love Him,
because we want to serve Him
until we see Him face to face.
(The Christian Service Brigade's "Battalion Watchword")

Around 1960 our church plant entered a new phase. The Sunday school program had grown and grown until the Southside Mission was larger than the mother church. At that point, some tension developed between the two entities, and eventually the leader of the mission led the people who were coming for Sunday school to merge with the Church of the Open Bible. Helen and I joined them, and soon afterwards I became a board member of the church.

Helen and I immediately saw a special need to minister to boys. I heard about a new organization that followed the general idea of Boy Scouts but was based on evangelical Christianity. It was called the Christian Service Brigade (CSB), and it was for boys ages twelve to eighteen. I told the church board about the program, and they asked if I would be willing to start a local battalion. I agreed and began serving as "captain" and training others, including the older boys (sixteen to eighteen years old), to become leaders as well. Many of them thrived and remained faithful leaders throughout their lives, not only in this but also in many other areas of life. Our own son Stuart later became a captain as well.

I served as captain with CSB from 1959 to 1966, and then as area director until 1974. During that time, it was my great joy to see many boys put their faith in Jesus. One young man named Jimmy Whiteman came to the CSB when he was twelve years old. One day, I was met by a very boisterous group when I arrived. Someone had gotten hurt, and it happened to be the pastor's son. One of the sergeants was being blamed for the injury, and I had to help the sergeants work through their frustrations over what had happened.

Christian Service Brigade Captain, 1961

While I was doing this, Jimmy asked if he could see me. It wasn't convenient with the commotion that was going on, but the Lord led me to spend some time alone with him anyway. I asked him where he was at in his relationship with the Lord, and he told me he had been memorizing John 3:16. I asked him, "What do you want to do next?"

"I want to become a Christian," he replied. We talked a bit more about what being a Christian is all about, and that very day he knelt down to pray and accepted the Lord Jesus.

One of the most memorable experiences from my CSB years was a canoe trip that we organized for the boys in leadership training. The trip began on a bright, sunny day in late summer. Beginning near the town of Leader, we set out with three canoes, three teaching staff, and six teenage boys. There were several shallow sandbars to portage, so we had put in a good day by the time we came to Diefenbaker Lake on the Saskatchewan River. Our plan was to prepare supper and then spend the night there.

We had unloaded our supplies and were starting to get things together for supper when a severe wind started blowing. There were no trees or anything else for shelter. We couldn't start a fire with the wind howling, so we had to eat our hotdogs cold. When the wind got even stronger we discovered that there was no way we would be able to pitch our tents. "What in the world should we do now?" we wondered.

We decided, all nine of us, to huddle and pray. After praying earnestly for some time, we decided we would launch our canoes again. First we had to pack our gear back into the canoes. When we tried to launch the first canoe, though, we found ourselves facing right into a gale-force wind, and as we tried to get it through the waves breaking on the shore, it was swamped. We bailed the water out, and while six of us held the canoe in the water facing the wind, the three in the canoe started paddling and were able to make it out onto the lake. We launched the second canoe, with the same three holding and three more inside paddling. We saved the largest, deepest canoe for the last. Two men jumped in and started to paddle, and then the third jumped in. We worked hard, plowing through the waves. We got good and wet, but we were determined to reach the other shore, where we thought we saw a small sheltered hillside.

A third of the way across, the waves diminished and the storm weakened. By the time we had reached the middle of the lake, the wind stopped, the waves became smaller and smaller, and then all of a sudden the lake was as smooth as glass. Everyone was quiet as we brought the canoes together and said, "Thank You, Lord!"

Sometimes God creates a storm and puts us right in the middle of it. The brigade boys viewed it as a miracle, an extraordinary work of God that had strengthened all of our faith. The memories of this trip helped us build a strong brigade program to reach boys and girls, the highest percentage of whom were from non-churched homes.

Canoe trip on the Saskatchewan River, 1967

Soon we had a five-star leadership training program that was reaching the whole region. At one meeting, we had laymen and pastors from Shaunavon, Gull Lake, the Maple Creek area, Herbert and the surrounding rural area, and Swift Current. At another meeting, during the time that Rev. Don Merritt was the CSB president and I was the local area director, we talked about what it takes to have revival in our lives. We longed to see revival spread through the organization and the southwest.

The focus of our discussion was on having no unconfessed sin in our lives. As we were talking about this important theme, one of the teachers confessed his unforgiving attitude towards his pastor, who was sitting next to him, and toward another elder from the same church. They had a very emotional reconciliation, and the Holy Spirit spoke to everyone there. Everyone seemed to want to receive individual counseling, and our meeting lasted until after midnight. I believe that it was that revival that led to the great success of the CSB program in the following years, as many of the older teenage boys from our group went on to take on similar leadership roles in the next generation.

CHAPTER X

Bible College Student

If the LORD delights in a man's way, he makes his steps firm; though he stumble, he will not fall, for the LORD upholds him with his hand (Psalm 37:23–24).

Over the years, Hillcrest Shopping Centre had expanded as much as was possible on the corner lot. Our business, especially with Helen's bakeshop, had steadily increased. In fact, we had grown in volume until we were number one in sales among all the privately owned grocery stores in southwest Saskatchewan. Yet I was left with the strong feeling that there must be more. What could it be? A larger store? Our location did not permit further growth.

Then one day in the fall of 1964 I prayed, "Lord, if You cause the store to sell and help us, I'll attend a Bible college to learn more theology and have greater knowledge in counseling and teaching boys in the community." Well, in no time at all the Lord had answered that prayer! That same fall a buyer came along and paid cash for the store.

Once again, it was time for us to move. Our four children now ranged in age from four to sixteen, and in January of 1965 the six of us moved into a rented building on a farm near Swift Current. For me, it was like learning to walk by faith all over again. Many times we found peace in the saying "I know not what the future holds, but I know who holds the future in His hands."

Bible College student, 1965

At the age of forty, I was a student again! This time, though, I was studying at Millar Memorial Bible Institute. I studied theology, evangelism, the Pauline epistles, and other topics, mostly in classes taught by Herbert Peeler, who had allowed me to be a special student. Due to having four children, we had decided not to move to the campus until we had a clear sense of what God was calling us to do in ministry. Instead, I made many trips back and forth between Millar and Swift Current, one hour each way.

I studied hard and thoroughly enjoyed the time with other students. Herbert Peeler and his teaching had a profound effect on me, and I came to respect him very deeply. When a controversial topic came up in our class discussions or a student expressed a different view on some doctrine, Mr. Peeler would often say something like "You will have to decide what you want to believe. I have already established a view, and that is what we teach here and believe in." Mr. Peeler provided an opportunity for each of us students to grow and develop into a useful servant leader of the Lord.

While we were at Millar, a missionary leader and friend asked, "Will you plan to take on a new church plant in northern Saskatchewan?" Helen and I prayed but did not sense God leading us in that direction. In fact, we were presented with this opportunity twice, but neither time was there any indication that this was what God wanted us to do.

"Trust in the Lord *with all your heart and lean not on your own understanding; in all your ways acknowledge him, and he will make your paths straight"* (Proverbs 3:5–6).

When God led us to free ourselves from our business responsibilities and devote some time to studying the Bible more deeply, we had no other plans but to prepare ourselves better for some sort of ministry. There were times when I prayed, "Lord, You know I am not gifted in speaking; I would do a lousy job of that."

One day, a missionary statesman came along, Dr. Don Schidler of GMU. We traveled together back and forth from Swift Current to the Bible college over the course of three or four days. He was speaking at a Boy's Brigade service in Swift Current and teaching a series at Millar at the same time. So we had lots of time to visit together. I mentioned my dilemma to him, telling him that up until that point I had not felt God's call on my life to go into a specific ministry. I wondered what all of this Bible college training could be for if it wasn't for full-time ministry.

One day, at our last meeting together, Don said, "I know many men whom God has called to be in the business world or to run a business. Is it possible that God is calling you to be His ambassador in the business world? If you pray, God will direct you." When I did pray, I felt certain this was God's path for me, and Helen was willing to follow.

Where, though, were we to begin? Where should we go? After much prayer and many confirmations from the Lord, I realized that He wanted us to stay in Swift Current and continue our ministry with boys. So that would be our ministry focus, but what about the business part? After much exploring, we were given the answer to that question as well.

CHAPTER XI

Following God's Call

Freedom lies not in conforming to the world's expectations or even realizing what we take to be our deepest wishes; it lies in following the call on our lives (*Charles Colson, The Good Life*).

L ooking back, it would be easy to second-guess our decision to leave everything behind and head off to study the Bible. Should I have kept the store? Should I have launched my own cookware sales organization? Either of these options would have been "wise" in all sorts of ways, but neither was what God intended for me and Helen. In the end, I also saw that full-time ministry was not God's intention. I was to earn my living through business and continue to devote myself to God's work as well. What, though, would our business look like now that we had sold the store?

The answer came through a conversation with a neighbor who was manufacturing a product called a chaff blower, which could be mounted on a harvester combine. He suggested one day, "I'll sell you this product line and show you how to make them. I know you can do this; I watched you run the store. You and your family will do well in manufacturing."

Well, I looked his shop over and immediately thought, "This is a blacksmith shop, and this business involves working with steel." I went home and said to Helen, "You know, I can build a much better shop than that business has, and I can improve on their approach to manufacturing." Those words were to shape our lives for the next forty-six years.

With the challenge before us, my competitive spirit once again kicked into high gear. There was no shortage of enthusiasm as Helen and I began by building a new shop. It was a 40' by 40' Nelson home kit. We were starting over yet again, so my brother Peter put up the money for the shop. He was the owner of the building, and we rented the new shop from him.

We began with next to nothing, no equipment to speak of—only a few jigs, a few samples, a few drawings, and memories of how God had been faithful in the past and allowed me to be successful in sales. I told Helen and the children, "We'll work as a family to begin." By that time, Stan and Stuart were teenagers, and they were more than willing to help. And so, in January of 1966, with just our family and the bare necessities in equipment, we began manufacturing chaff blowers. Rem Manufacturing had been launched!

First Rem shop on the west side of Swift Current, 1966

Rem's first new product, a vac feed blower

"My son, do not despise the LORD's discipline and do not resent his rebuke, because the LORD disciplines those he loves, as a father the son he delights in" (Proverbs 3:11–12).

We believed then, and we believe now, that we were following the call of God on our lives when we started manufacturing farm machinery. Because it was God's call, it was God's work. And we were pleased to be about whatever business the Lord assigned to us.

Stan Rempel, 1965

The new business gave us a way to provide for our family and also taught us to work together as a family. Our oldest son, Stanley James, was our first employee at age eighteen, and over the years many family members would be involved in the business. Although his time at Rem was fairly short, as

73

God had other plans for him and his wife, Zelda, Stan still speaks often about the times when he installed chaff blowers on combine thrashers.

Stuart started off working part-time at Rem after school and during summer months. After university he worked for Rem for ten years before he and his wife, Joellen, felt God's call into ministry. Connie also came to help at Rem in her early teen years and joined me in taking flying lessons. After college, Connie and her husband, Lorne Dennis, both worked for Rem and developed strong leadership and management skills. Jane also helped at Rem at an early age and was known for how quickly she learned new skills. In college, Jane met her husband, Bob Sonntag, and they came to Rem in 1984. Bob helped in sales, both Canadian and American, and also in administration. Jane and Bob are still with Rem Enterprises today.

Connie Rempel, 1979 *Jane Rempel, 1973* *Leann Rempel, 1987*

Our fifth child, Leann, who was born nine years after Jane and started work much later than our other children, became the "artist" at Rem, excelling in drafting and design. She was always a fast learner and helped a lot in sales and sales management. Leann served as my assistant for many years and helped make many management decisions. She is still serving in management positions at Rem today and living in Swift Current with her husband, Duaine, and their children, Theo and Dani.

Our older grandchildren have also played roles in the company. Christopher (Connie's son) studied at SIAST and began his career at Rem in information technology. Mike (Jane's son) also began his career in computer technology and worked with Rem for a number of years, in both sales and management. For a time he served as the manager of our plant in the U.S. What a talented family God gave us! And what a blessing it has been to have so many of them involved in the business He called us to start.

Our central purpose as we built our business remained honoring God one day at a time. We continued training boys in the community and encouraging many to become better leaders. I was now much better equipped to teach after four months of intensive study at Millar, and the Christian Service Brigade program continued to grow in Swift Current and the surrounding area.

We began to invest heavily in another area of ministry, in terms of time, energy, and finances. As a board member of the Church of the Open Bible, I heard about the unhappy state of the church's manse (pastor's residence). It was so run down that it had no sales value. Who would want to buy such a place? To help out, Helen and I decided to buy the manse and rebuild it ourselves.

We were in our first year of manufacturing and very busy with the business. We could not expect sales, and the cash flow that came with them, until the summer months. So Helen and I decided to repair and then move into the old manse. This decision, flowing out of a sincere desire to help our church, would ultimately lead to another tragedy—a tragedy that I was only able to survive with the Lord's intervention and strength.

> You talk of faith when you're up on the mountain.
> Oh but the talk comes easy when life's at its best.
> But it's down in the valley of trials and temptation
> That's when faith is really put to the test.

> For the God on the mountain is still God in the valley.
> When things go wrong, He'll make it right.
> And the God of the good times is still God in the bad times.
> The God of the day is still God in the night.
> (From "God On the Mountain" by Tracy G. Dartt)

We were expecting a heavy rain shower in early June 1966, and I was busy preparing a drainpipe on the second story of the manse. The ladder was standing on the patio, and our two boys were holding it in place. It began to rain, and there was lightning. I called down, "I've got it done!" and went to climb down the ladder with some tools in my hand.

Suddenly the ladder shifted on the wet concrete patio. It slipped backwards and went crashing down, with me hanging on to the top. As I fell, my throat hit one of the ladder rungs, and then my chin smashed into the concrete patio. My left side had also collided with the side rail of the ladder.

I was in bad shape. Stan and Stuart helped rush me to the hospital. The x-rays showed that I had seven broken bones in my head, a severe neck injury, an injured leg, and a damaged voice box, throat, and elbow. The doctor did the only thing he knew how to do: he gave me morphine and put me to sleep. He went to a party and told the people there that he had no idea what to do with me.

The next day, my oldest brother came to see me. I was bleeding from my mouth and couldn't move. The swelling continued to get worse, and after more delays I was sent to Regina by car, with a big shot of morphine to help me make the trip. In the midst of the pain—pain unlike any I had experienced before—I prayed. "Lord, You suffered far more than I am suffering from this accident. Now I can begin to understand what You suffered for me and for many others. Thank You for being willing to go through that to save us from our sins."

When I was finally sent home, Helen not only had the task of cooking and caring for our family and helping at Rem; she now also had me to take care of. And then we were faced with a difficult realization: Sales depended on me, and I couldn't speak or even move my mouth. The only way I could eat was to drink through a straw. We prayed, "Lord, will You send us a helper? We're not able to carry on by ourselves."

As in the past, God again sent someone along at just the right time. David Gunther was a godly Christian man. He came to us one day and said, "I believe I can help you. I understand the valuable contribution your product can make to farmers, and I'm a salesman." Wow! He seemed to be a fine young man. He went on, "I married one of your neighbor's daughters, and that's what has brought me to the area. I have the time it will take to sell your product." Again, wow! What a gracious God we serve! He who had called us to start this business was showing Himself faithful to give us what we needed to take it forward, even in the midst of the most challenging trials.

And so 1966, the first year of the business for Rem Manufacturing, came to a close. It was time to assess how we were doing and to think and pray about what to do next. As we prayed about it, God brought us to the realization that we needed to get fully in line with what He was calling us to do and to be. Rem, the business, and Frank, the servant of Jesus, needed to run parallel courses from here on. Both had to have the same purpose. Goals had to be set for each, and those goals needed to be pursued with great enthusiasm.

The purpose for both me as an individual and Rem was always to be the same: to honor God one day at a time. As the business grew in the years ahead, we recognized that God had called us to this business and given us success so we could help to fulfill the Great Commission to go and make disciples of all nations, teaching them to obey everything Jesus had commanded. Recognizing Rem as part of the calling God had given us shaped the value system that was the foundation of our business. We were doing the work our Heavenly Father had given us to do. So we approached it joyfully, with integrity and character, and with our central desire being to honor God in our business and our family relationships, and through our giving to help fulfill the Great Commission.

"Your word is a lamp to my feet and a light for my path"
(Psalm 119:105).

As a counselor at a Billy Graham Crusade in the local hockey auditorium, I saw my neighbor Lee Lamb, a Chinese businessman, go forward after a service in which Leighton Ford was preaching. I followed him to the front, and we greeted each other. I asked him if he had any questions that I could help him with. In broken English he told me, "I received a Bible some years ago. After reading it, I understood that I must be born again, but I was never obedient to God. I'm wondering, what does it mean where Jesus says, 'I am the bread of life'?"

I responded, "You're a storekeeper. Your customers often come to buy a fresh loaf of bread. That bread is a staple food, something we need every

ABOUT OUR FATHER'S BUSINESS

day. In the same way, you need Jesus at the center of your life every day in order to have an abundant, fruitful Christian life." Lee Lamb went on to become a founding member of the Chinese church in town.

Some time later, when Helen and I were invited to the baptism of three members of his family (representing three generations) at his church, he told me, "Ninety percent of my family have now become believers. Three generations have followed Jesus by being baptized." When Lee Lamb chose to follow Jesus, a revival came to his family as they watched the change in him. He lived to see his 100th birthday, diligently following the Lord to the very end of his life.

God was always bringing people—boys, men, and families—into our lives so we could help them to clearly understand what God had done for them and how He wanted them to know, serve, and honor Him. He often brought hitchhikers across our path, and we had the privilege of seeing many of them respond positively to God's call to repent and turn to Him for salvation.

But now, with my voice gone, I could no longer teach or share the gospel. I wondered what He had in store for me now. I had been handicapped at age thirty-two by carbon monoxide poisoning, and now, at age forty-two, it had happened again. My broken bones were painful, but the damage done to my voice was even more challenging. Speaking above a whisper was almost impossible, but it had the benefit of forcing me to learn how to communicate more gently and with fewer words. This would prove helpful as I stepped into new leadership roles in the years ahead.

> Moses said to the LORD, "O Lord, I have never been eloquent, neither in the past nor since you have spoken to your servant. I am slow of speech and tongue." The LORD said to him, "Who gave man his mouth? Who makes him deaf or mute? Who gives him sight or makes him blind? Is it not I, the LORD?" (Exodus 4:10–11)

Moses was a lowly shepherd when God called him. He was working for his father-in-law, Jethro. When God told Moses that He was sending him to lead His people out of Egypt, Moses essentially responded, "I'm nobody. I can't do it!" Before he left Egypt Moses had thought quite highly of himself. He believed that God had raised him up to do the very thing God was now asking of him (see Acts 7:23–25). God's response was to send him out into the wilderness for forty years so that he could recognize his own insufficiency. It was only after Moses came to a point of not trusting in himself and his own abilities that God called him to the work He had for him. What a story! Moses was qualified for the job only after he realized he couldn't do it!

When God called, I had become chairman of the board at our church. Prior to my accident, we had been attempting to plan and build a new church. Now, it was time to take up that challenge. Once again, we looked to God to meet our needs, and He again provided in an extraordinary way. The old church had been built on a business lot on Main Street, and that lot was now quite valuable. When we found an interested buyer, the negotiations began. The church board had agreed that if we could get fifty percent of the funds needed to build the new church we would sell the old one. After some dickering the buyer finally came to within $4000 of our needed amount, but they wouldn't go a dollar higher. It didn't look like we were going to reach our target and be able to build the new church; but then the Lord gave me an idea. I pointed out to the potential buyer that once they owned the property they would need to remove the old church before they could build, and it would be costly to do so. I, of course, could help them with that. We eventually settled on a fee for tearing down the old church: $4000! That meant the money was in place for building the new church, but we still had the task and expense of demolishing the old church. Here, too, the Lord provided. We were able to find a man who was willing to do the work with his only payment being the salvaged material from the old church.

Despite this seeming success, there was also criticism. Some said I was too aggressive, and these complaints were a great test for me. But God sent encouragement at just the right time. Helen and I received a letter from Victoria, BC, from two well-to-do founding members of the church who had retired and moved away. They knew Helen and me well and were very familiar with our involvement in the Christian Service Brigade. They wrote, "We prayed for many years that God would send a leader to the church. When we heard that you were chairman of the board, we knew that God had answered those prayers." Their words of encouragement came just when the accident and other tensions were making me want to quit. Like Moses, I realized that I was not up to the task, but God's strength was more than sufficient, and He was encouraging me to press on despite the challenges and opposition. By God's grace, we dedicated the new church building in the fall of 1968, complete with a Rem-made spire, which is still visible and standing today in 2013.

In those days, there seemed to be no end of opportunities for this man that God had brought through the wilderness. I didn't feel qualified for any of them, but I had come to understand that when a branch is well-connected to the Vine, it is able to bear much fruit. That was exactly what I wanted to do, serve God one day at a time in whatever way He chose and bring Him as much glory as I could.

CHAPTER XII

About Our Father's Business

On my bed I remember you; I think of you through the watches of the night...My soul clings to you; your right hand upholds me (Psalm 63:6–8).

I n those early years of building a new company, there were always new challenges and new things that required someone who could handle the task. God regularly gave me a driving ambition to do things that were far bigger than I could handle alone, and He also always brought the right help at the right time. My brother David, who had been helping to build our products, was unable to continue doing so, but our son Stanley came to help. Helen served as our bookkeeper. God had given her a gift of being able to keep all of the details straight and in order.

Our first hired staff member was John Bartsch, who was my sister Ann's husband and proved to be invaluable. John was both an engineer and a craftsman, and he quickly became my design helper. Together we designed a new model of the chaff blower and a dump wagon in 1967. More importantly, that year we also designed and launched our first completely new product—a vacuum feed blower. It was a great success, and Rem made a good profit that year, only our second year in business.

As the Lord continued to give strength and bless our business, we made plans for a new building. All of the times of testing seemed to be fading into the background, but we would never forget how God had intervened so many times on our behalf.

David Rempel, 1966

Rem's first employee, John Bartsch, in 2005

In 1968, we built a brand new 6,500 square foot building, and Rem experienced a banner year. Our business grew quickly, and so did our staff. We were now located on South Railway Street with a new building, new equipment, and a much larger group of men to help meet the growing demand for our products.

The next year, in the early spring of 1969, Helen and I traveled to Kansas to meet with other manufacturers to explore exporting our products. Exporting would prove to serve a critical role in the growth of Rem in the years ahead. In fact, the export market had much to do with our story of success, with the American market quickly coming to represent two-thirds of our sales volume, a level that continues until today in 2013.

"The righteous will live by faith" (Romans 1:17).

In every dream or vision, there is emotion that leads to action. First comes the dream and the passion to pursue it. Dreams and passion are not enough, though. They have to be followed by a great deal of planning and time invested in exploring a variety of possible opportunities. It takes plenty of patience and a lot of hard work to bring the dream to fruition.

Most important of all, though, is prayer. We wanted to proceed by faith, not by our own ingenuity. We recognized that Rem was God's idea, not ours, and for all of the details of what He had in mind to be realized we would need to seek guidance in every situation before doing anything else. I found that the best time to do this was early in the morning when my mind was still uncluttered by the demands of the busy day ahead. The fuller our schedule became, the more we recognized that prayer needed to be our first priority. It's much like driving a car. When you drive, it's very important to decide which direction you're going to go before putting the car into gear. Backing out of your garage doesn't work very well when the car is in "drive"! The same is true in life. It's always a good idea to put your mind into gear before opening your mouth.

Anyone who knows me will tell you that I seem to have a new idea every hour. Not all of them, though, are good ideas or God's ideas. We knew that we needed to carefully examine my ideas before moving forward. We had many questions we would ask ourselves. Would this dream be worth the price? Or might the price be too much to pay? Was it really God's plan for us, or just our own dream? Would the dream fit with our commitment to honoring God one day at a time? If we followed the dream, would it rob us of all our time and energy and ultimately harm our family relationships? We were not opposed to sacrifices—sacrifice had been our life—but we knew that God expected us to care for the children He had blessed us with.

Most of all, as we sought to "drive" our business forward, we recognized how critical it was to be sure that God had told us what direction to go before making any significant moves. We found that God was very gracious to direct us as we prayed. He would speak to us through His Word, through the peace that He brought about a particular course of action, through advice and support from loved ones, and in a variety of other ways. Once we were confident that we had His stamp of approval, we were ready to move forward and work toward making the dream a reality. With God's leading, we were ready to invest the necessary time and resources and also to say no to other commitments that might undermine achieving what God had directed us to do.

"Jesus replied: 'Love the Lord your God with all your heart and with all your soul and with all your mind'" (Matthew 22:37).

When we moved our business in 1968 and expanded our operations, we found that the sales and marketing department needed to move ahead faster than they had been. As we wrestled with the uncertainties of how to move forward, I learned another very important lesson. "The dream may be good, but the timing bad." That seemed to be what had happened in this case.

We had taken a major step forward as a business just before an economic downturn that we could not have anticipated. I remember that during this time, in March of 1969, Helen and I took another trip to Kansas. Our show equipment had been sent ahead, and it was just the two of us together for the long drive down. On the way, we had plenty of time to evaluate our situation. We were expecting our fifth child in midsummer. For the business to thrive, my traveling days were necessarily increasing. We needed to increase sales, and we would need to hire, train, and manage more personnel for the larger shop. We would also need to develop new machinery if we were going to survive.

Our beautiful daughter Leann came into our lives on August 1, 1969. She immediately became our pride and joy. We were so fortunate to have a bright, healthy daughter nine years after gaining our lovely "singing with joy" daughter (Jane). Our family was our treasure. We considered ourselves very fortunate to have the business that God called us to, and working together as a family was one of our goals. For this to happen, though, our business needed to succeed.

CHAPTER XIII

The Marriage of Business and Ministry

"Love your neighbor as yourself" (Matthew 22:39).

As we thought and prayed about our circumstances, we became convinced that marketing our products in the U.S. was the one hope for our future. This is where we decided to focus our energy; this became our new dream, and it proved to be the right choice.

In early March 1970, I decided to attend the 3-I Show (Industry, Implements, and Irrigation) in Dodge City, Kansas. We had designed and built a forty-foot goose neck trailer. We filled the trailer with equipment and pulled it with a one-tonne truck.

As I entered South Dakota, I saw a sign that read "Speed Limit 40 mph." After a while, I came to another sign that read "End of Speed Zone." At that point, I sped up to fifty-five miles per hour again, the standard speed on the highway, but I soon noticed that I was being followed by a car. I couldn't think of why that car would be obviously following me until lights started flashing.

I stopped. The officer said I was speeding, and he wanted me to drive into town and stop at the sheriff's office. When we got there, he told me that I had been going fifty-five miles per hour in a forty miles per hour zone. I told him, "No, there was a sign that said 'End of Speed Zone.'" But he insisted that there was no such sign!

It was 11:00 p.m., and he gave me the choice of paying the eighty-five dollar fine or going before a judge in a few days. To compound things, I had heard on the radio about a storm that was coming, and I knew I had very little time to get to Kansas before the storm hit. I wasn't carrying very much cash—since I didn't have much to carry!—but I decided I had better pay the fine and get back on the road while I could. This left me with almost no cash for the rest of the trip. I later found out that almost every truck was caught in that speed trap, and most of them would pay the fine even though they knew it was a trap set by local police, rather than taking the time and expense to hire a lawyer and challenge the fine.

As I drove south, the snow began to fall. By morning the snow was too deep on the road for me to keep going. I wasn't sure what to do but decided to wait for a big semi-truck, and when one came along I followed it.

I was able to make it to a town in Nebraska, but at that point I could go no farther. Everyone who was traveling had to wait for the snowplows to clear the roads. After a while, two snowplows came along, and as they went ahead I followed slowly behind with a long line of truckers. The snowflakes were as big as butterflies. They were very pretty but not very practical—and they just kept coming. By that time, the snow on the highway was over twelve inches deep.

After many hours of slow travel, we arrived near the Kansas border, and there was a long hill to climb. The snow had piled up on the trailer and my load was very heavy. Halfway up the hill, with a steep drop-off on my side of the road, I began losing traction. I was getting ready to give up and jump when I had the good sense to pray first and ask the Lord to help me.

After praying, I decided to try to move into the lane coming from the other direction, since there was no traffic on that side; and as soon as I did I was able to gain enough traction to keep going. I made it up the hill on the wrong side of the highway and said, "Thank You, Lord!" Once again God had graciously intervened at my moment of need.

The snow stopped, the temperature grew warmer, and then the snow began to melt. It turned into a sunny, pleasant afternoon as I reached the border of Kansas. I was tempted to drive through to my destination, but a sign said for truckers to report for a permit. I knew I did not have enough cash for a permit, so I prayed to the Lord to help me. I had no idea what to do.

When I walked into the office, the officer on duty asked me what I was hauling. I told him I had a load of farm machinery for the 3-I Show. He informed me that I was exempt, so I left and kept going! God had heard my prayer and answered. Once again I had to say, "Thank You, Lord!"

The one-tonne truck was a bit cramped to sleep in, and the cab was not very big, but I would make do. I had enough cash left to buy a quart of orange juice and a box of whole wheat crackers. The temperature in Dodge City was seventy-two degrees that day, the sun was shining, and I ended up with quite a sunburn.

Despite the challenges of getting there and my meager accommodations and rations, the show was very busy and interesting. While there I met a dealer by the name of Paul Dopps. He had a broken leg and was using a crutch to help him walk. I brought him a chair, and we sat down to visit. We immediately became friends. He said that his son was looking after his display and would call him if he needed him. He told me that he believed he could sell my machinery if I was looking for a dealer and invited me to join him for dinner that night at his hotel restaurant. When he asked where my hotel was, I told him my hotel was my truck! He graciously invited me to share the room that his son was staying in.

That evening I asked Paul, "If something were to happen to me and you, would I see you in heaven?"

He responded by telling me a story: "I was quiet when I got married. My wife was a strong Catholic, and we became a well-to-do family; we didn't lack anything. But I couldn't adjust to her religion, so I pursued other things. One day, I was invited to a men's retreat sponsored by Campus Crusade for Christ. At the retreat, I heard the gospel message and decided to repent of my sins and embrace Jesus as my Lord and Savior. What a blessing it was to know that I now had eternal life! I was full of joy and went home and told my wife what had happened to me. Well, she saw this new way of life that I had chosen as being against her religion, and she was not impressed at all. But I could not give up what I had found; nor could I adjust to her church. Soon she took our children and left me, and she cleaned me out financially. Despite all of this, I was at peace. I had come to know God personally! I had started a new life and now would make a new beginning in business. At times I have struggled with all of the changes in my life and missing my family. And on top of all the challenges, not long ago I had an accident that broke my leg. My oldest son recently came to stay with me, and that has helped me a lot."

My friend was discouraged by all that had happened to him since he became a follower of Jesus. I sensed his deep need and wanted to help him, so I arranged for us to attend an evangelical church on Sunday morning before the show started. The Lord ministered powerfully to my new friend, and he left the church service with new joy in the Lord and a new resolve to walk in close fellowship with God.

"But seek first his kingdom and his righteousness, and all these things will be given to you as well" (Matthew 6:33).

As it turned out, I spent nearly all of my time in Dodge City with Paul Dopps. That was certainly not what I expected of this trip, but God had more in mind than I could have guessed. He wanted me to minister to this brother in Christ who needed encouragement. What about the much needed sale of our Rem machinery? Well, somehow it was all sold or designated to be sold, and I came home with the cash we needed. Rem was able to keep going again, and we had the promise of more export sales to come. I had been obedient to what I believed God had called me to do, minister to a needy person. I've learned that when we follow God's leading, we can leave the consequences to him. As I sought first His kingdom, God graciously intervened on our behalf and took care of our business needs, one day at a time. When I left Dodge City, I not only had gained a new friend and sold the equipment I needed to sell, I had also gained a U.S. distributor for our products!

Helen and I were continuing to see how God's calling to build a business was His way for us to have broader impact in being His ambassadors. We learned that God delights to use our efforts to reach out to others, whether it is those we meet in our business ventures and travels or those close to home, including our own families.

These opportunities continued to increase as we designed new products and improved our product line and our business continued to grow. One of the new product lines was a plot harvester intended for research stations, universities, and export to other countries. Around that time, we began to export products to Japan as well.

Helen and I traveled to Pearl Harbor in Oahu, Hawaii, in 1975 to meet with our Japanese importer and his friend. We ate lots of Japanese food over the course of two days, with negotiations taking place through a translator. Eventually I realized that we were experiencing a clash of cultures. In my culture, when trying to make a deal I would give my best price and stick to it. I was learning that in Japanese culture people never paid the asking price. There was always negotiation, and people were not satisfied unless they got a discount. Had I known this, I would have raised the price a bit to begin with and then given them the "discount" that would have satisfied them. In the end, I had to tell them that I had already given them my best, lowest price, and I was sorry that we would not be able to reach an agreement.

But I wanted to seize the opportunity to be God's witness. I said, "I have to explain our culture to you. Helen and I are Christians. We have accepted God's free gift of eternal life by receiving Jesus as our Lord and Savior. We love God and believe that you have become our friends. So we want to show you what helped us to believe. We want to give you this book, called *The Way*. It will explain to you the way to know God and teach you about the Christian culture that we have adopted." I showed them where a good place would be to begin reading and then told them, "Although we will be staying here for a few more days, we won't need to meet again. Thank you for coming to Hawaii to meet with us."

Later that day, the Japanese businessman called and said he wished to meet with us again. They brought Helen a gift and said they wished to buy us an American steak dinner that night. We enjoyed visiting with them, and everyone seemed to have a good time. After dinner they handed us an envelope and said, "Please look at what we gave you." When we opened the envelope, we saw that it contained a purchase order for plot harvesters at the price we had been asking. The deal was done, and there was no further negotiation required.

In the end, Helen and I had both a wonderful vacation time and a very successful trip. We always wondered what would have happened if we had not shared our testimony of faith with them. Would we have received the order? They later told us they had been reading the book we gave them, and we did business with them for many years afterwards. Our relationship was marked by trust and cooperation. We knew that God had once again intervened and helped Rem to continue and become a successful business enterprise. "We know not what the future holds, but we know who holds the future in His hands."

In my travels to see customers, I had the privilege of meeting many interesting people. On one occasion, I visited with the president of the Morris Rod Weeder Company, Mr. George Morris. He showed me a spring-type harrow tine and said he wished we made them in western Canada. I asked him how many he needed, as I immediately saw this as another opportunity. I also asked if I could have a sample.

We began the process of learning how to manufacture and heat-treat or stress-relieve oil-tempered spring wire. All of the learning, gathering information, setting up the manufacturing process, and building the tools to manufacture the springs took only a few months. We bought a used cookstove and heated the oven to maximum temperature. We used a time-temperature method of stress relieving by testing the wear life and comparing it with the sample. We were able to begin to supply the Morris Company with harrow tines in no time at all.

Soon we improved our manufacturing equipment for high-volume production. When there was a request for larger harrow tines, we made what we called a tapered coil that would become our quality, long-life, superior harrow tine as business continued to grow. Rem Manufacturing became the major western Canadian supplier for harrow tines for the agricultural industry, with markets in Canada, the USA, Australia and Europe. This part of Rem is still operating today, with 300 varieties of hay rake and baler teeth and an ever-increasing supply of harrow tines, including larger sizes.

"May the words of my mouth and the meditation of my heart be pleasing in your sight, O LORD, my Rock and my Redeemer" (Psalm 19:14).

During these years, even as Rem was growing and expanding, Helen and I were also growing in important ways in our relationship with Jesus Christ and in our role as His ambassadors. In 1971, we went on a brief vacation to Banff, Alberta. We had heard about a weekend retreat called the Lay Institute for Evangelism that was hosted by Bill Bright from California.

At this retreat, Helen and I made the wonderful discovery of the Spirit-filled life (see Appendix 2). This involved being filled with the Holy Spirit and living constantly, moment by moment, under His gracious direction. It meant intentionally getting off the throne of our lives and daily yielding to Jesus' control. When we do this, we are empowered by the Holy Spirit to live as God intended. Our prayer life becomes joyful and effective, we increasingly introduce others to Jesus, we understand God's Word more and more, we grow in obedience to Christ and trust Him more fully, and the fruit of the Spirit fills our lives. After the retreat, we found ourselves filled with joy in doing door-to-door evangelism, and we now had the ability to forgive those who acted dishonestly toward us in business.

As we shared what we had learned with others, God blessed us by bringing fruit through our testimonies and teaching. This was particularly evident in my role with the Christian Service Brigade. Some years prior to this they had asked me to be the area director for the southwest of Saskatchewan, helping to train adult leaders and organize rallies. As I shared about the Spirit-filled life, I had the joy of seeing revival come to the twenty-six CSB leaders in training.

A year later, I became involved with the Christian Business Men's Committee (CBMC). My primary role was helping with outreach among high school graduates. Again, God graciously brought fruit as I lived as a branch connected to the Vine and filled with the Spirit.

Then, in 1973, the leaders of the Associated Gospel Churches denomination (AGC) asked me to serve on their executive board. I had the privilege of being the only layperson serving with a bunch of pastors on the board for western Canada. One of my roles was to organize the AGC lay-leader retreats. In 1974, I became a board member for Millar Memorial Bible Institute just when the leader, Mr. Peeler, became ill. The following year I was appointed chairman of the board, and I would serve in that role until 1991.

In 1975, I was asked to lead Campus Crusade's "I found it!" campaign in Swift Current and area and also to serve on the provincial committee. In all of these endeavors, seeing people's lives changed kept me going, as did the knowledge that we were helping to fulfill the Great Commission.

Reaching the world with the Good News of Jesus Christ was the driving force in our lives. But the combination of responsibilities at Rem and serving in a variety of ministry roles made heavy demands on my time and had some unexpected consequences.

CHAPTER XIV

Family, Business, and Ministry

Who can discern his errors? Forgive my hidden faults. Keep your servant also from willful sins; may they not rule over me (Psalm 19:12–13).

The decisions that I made at this stage of my life had a direct impact on our family life. Our goal always was to work together as a family, but involvement in the business took time away from more normal family time and weakened, rather than strengthened, our relationships with one another. We had wrongly put too much confidence in the activities of our local church, where I was heavily involved, to help our children grow strong in the Lord. We did not see the dangers of being so busy or how our overly full lives were impacting our relationships with each other and with our precious children. Plain and simple, I needed to be home more.

When my busy schedule kept me away, Helen always took over and carried the load of organizing and making sure the needs of our children were looked after. She has always been my loyal, dedicated, supportive wife. No one else that I know could have handled Helen's workload and still led our family well when my agenda took me away from home.

When family pressures increased, Helen and I both found daily renewal, thanks to what we had learned during our time at the Lay Institute for Evangelism and a personal meeting with Dr. Bill Bright. But we still found ourselves often asking the question: How can we help our children find the peace, love and joy that we have? We tried in so many ways to teach them.

Some of our children were struggling in their relationships with the Lord, and we began giving more time to them, seeking help from others, and devoting ourselves more to prayer. Their struggles significantly damaged their lives, and we wrestled as parents when we could not find the answers to help them. We often felt overwhelmed, as our children seemed to make one bad choice after another.

As we prayed, God came to our rescue. He reminded us that although we do not know what the future holds, we know who holds the future in His hands. When all our efforts to help our children failed, we still could trust that God was at work and had a good plan for their future. As Helen and I spent more time in prayer, we increasingly came to understand that God would never fail us, but His timing is often quite different than ours. The future belongs to Him; He is in charge, not us. He knows best, not us.

We wondered, though, whether we could have helped our children more if we had not been so busy. Should we give up Rem, the business God had called us to build? These questions were heavy on our hearts, and Helen and I took time off to find answers.

As we were praying, meditating, and talking with our children, Leann was playing her little tape player. One song kept catching our attention, and God used it to speak to us: "So for my sake, teach me to take one day at a time." We came back home from our retreat energized. We felt that God had provided an answer—we were to continue both Rem and our ministries, but we also needed to invest more energy in our family.

Piper Arrow with Stuart and Leann, 1975

I was on the road quite a lot in those days, trying to sell our products and maintain good relationships with our customers. To try to minimize my time away, I decided to get my pilot's license. At first flight training was simply another time-consuming activity, but after graduation in 1974 I started flying my own Piper Arrow and could be home in the evenings more often. Business at Rem continued to increase, our staff was always expanding, and Helen was busy keeping our accounts in good order while I sold our products and sought to take our business forward.

If we could do things over again, we would definitely choose to spend more time investing in our children and especially helping them navigate the challenges of their teen years. But by the late 1970s, four of our five children had grown to adulthood, with only Leann still a child. At that point, we thought that if we could find a farm with horses, it would give us some wholesome activities to do as a family and help keep us together. So in 1979 we bought an eighty-eight-acre farm one mile south of Swift Current. Along with the farm, we bought some quarter horses. The farm became a very special place for Leann, in particular, and later for our grandchildren. They would come and work on the farm throughout the summer, swimming, fishing, and having a good time.

The farm, 1984

CHAPTER XV

Adventures in Flying

For he will command his angels concerning you to guard you in all your ways; they will lift you up in their hands (Psalm 91:11–12).

On a bright, sunny day in 1976, I came to the small town of Harvey, North Dakota. It was 12:30 p.m. as I flew over the runway, and I noticed that I would be landing on a gravel surface. I came around and lowered my speed to the slowest possible for my Piper Arrow. I was alone in the plane.

Just before touchdown I saw a pile of gravel on the runway. The gravel pile was only visible from ground level, and I was now too close to pull up and too low to clear it. I quickly cried out, "Help me, Lord!" and pulled hard, 40 percent flap. Then I heard a bang!

The plane's landing wheels hit the gravel pile, but instead of crashing the plane kept going down the runway. Slowly it came to a stop. I looked over the landing gear carefully, but no damage had been done. Then I went to look at the gravel pile and saw the clear marks where the landing gear had hit the gravel.

Impossible! There was no way the plane could have hit that pile of gravel and not summersaulted, but somehow the plane and I were not hurt in any way. Apparently the runway contractor had left for lunch, and a gravel truck had simply dumped a load of gravel instead of spreading it. It appeared that although the runway contractor was out to lunch, two angels were on the job, one at the end of each wing, lifting the plane over the hump! God had again intervened in my life and kept me safe. I thanked the Lord, finished my sales call, and then flew away to the next part of my journey.

"But God demonstrates his own love for us in this: While we were still sinners, Christ died for us" (Romans 5:8).

On another occasion, I was making a business call in Bismarck, North Dakota. Stuart was with me. After finishing our business we traveled by taxi to the airport where our Piper Arrow was parked. We had enough daylight hours left to reach Swift Current. Stuart had recently moved his family from St. Paul, Minnesota, back to Waldeck, near Swift Current, and was anxious to be home for the night.

Sitting in the passenger seat, I introduced myself to the young taxi driver and asked him if Bismarck was his hometown. He said no. He had come home from the Vietnam War not long before and was trying to adjust to civilian life. He had a friend in Bismarck, so he had decided to settle there. I asked him if he was at peace with himself and if he had plans for the future. He said no to both.

I asked if he had the confidence that he would be in heaven when he died and whether his family had taught him about God. Again he said no; that had not been part of his learning. I told him, "I have some wonderful news for you! Let me tell you about God, who loves you so much that He died for you. You can have the free gift of eternal life and know real peace." He asked me how that could be possible.

We arrived at the airport, and after I told him the Good News about Jesus Christ, he gladly said the sinner's prayer. I gave him a booklet to read and advised him to tell others who, like himself, needed a friend and a Savior. Our time together was brief, but God's Spirit was clearly at work in those moments.

"Have no fear of sudden disaster or of the ruin that overtakes the wicked, for the LORD will be your confidence and will keep your foot from being snared" (Proverbs 3:25–26).

Stuart and I took off from Bismarck, and about fifteen minutes into the flight the radio came alive: "You're approaching a squall front with severe winds and dark clouds, and you have very little time to land or to avoid it."

As I had already learned many years before, God sometimes creates a storm and then puts us in the storm. This storm was impressive! I asked the Minot Airport to give us a radar vector and guide us in. We had to fly by instruments, since visual flight was impossible. It became so dark from the storm that we could barely see the wings of our plane!

The flight controller in Minot advised us to climb to a higher altitude due to the severe turbulence and downdrafts. We were supposed to turn right ten degrees and after a few minutes turn to fifteen degrees and then slow our speed and turn on the flaps and lower our altitude.

Suddenly we broke through the clouds, and the runway was directly in front of us. We landed, took on more fuel, and then flew home. The squall was behind us. We both thanked the Lord, who had again graciously intervened for us.

We were faithful to be God's ambassadors to the taxi driver, even though it delayed our departure and resulted in us facing a terrible storm. God never promises that following the leading of His Spirit will take us around storms rather than through them. Someday, perhaps we will understand why so many storms came to our lives.

The Vietnam veteran was carrying a heavy burden, and he desperately needed the Lord. God ministered to him through us and then turned around and took care of us in our time of need. In all of it, He was accomplishing His good purposes as we chose to let Him direct our lives rather than doing it ourselves. Once again we were seeing how being in the business God had directed us to build allowed us to be about our Father's business. We wanted to obey the call of the Great Commission, and traveling on Rem business was allowing me to go into all the world to be a witness for Jesus.

We sometimes asked ourselves which was more important, the business call or the call to share God's Word. The answer is that both are important, because in our case God has called us to do both. Each of us must follow the path God sets before us and then seek to be His witness as we walk that path, whether it's in vocational ministry, as a businessman, as a farmer, or in whatever profession God leads us to.

So, if you think you are standing firm, be careful that you don't fall! No temptation has seized you except what is common to man. And God is faithful; he will not let you be tempted beyond what you can bear. But when you are tempted, he will also provide a way out so that you can stand up under it (1 Corinthians 10:12–13)

Not every encounter with people in my business travels, though, was as focused on the gospel as I would have liked. I recall the time I was traveling with two pastors. We flew at 9,000 feet over the south end of Lake Michigan and then landed the Piper Arrow at Sault Ste. Marie for fuel and a rest. The next morning we flew to Guelph, Ontario, and parked the Piper. I checked into a motel and ordered a rental car for an early morning business trip to Toronto.

After a very long day of meetings, I was back in Guelph for a night's rest. The next morning I took the car back to the rental agency and asked if they could give me a ride to the airport. The same young lady who had delivered the car said that she would take me. The next thing I knew, we were back at my hotel, parked in front of the room I had left. "Oh, I want to get to the airport, to my plane," I told her.

She replied, "I've got all day if you want." I insisted that I wanted to go to the local airport.

On the way there, I asked why she was looking for that type of relationship. She told me that she was a Satan worshiper, and she began recounting a strange story about parties with others in Guelph. I asked her why she worshiped Satan and was involved in the occult. She said, "There is power and a lot of excitement." She stopped the car in a park, but I told her to keep driving.

Then I began explaining to her how I had discovered that God loves me and how I got to know God personally. When we came to the airport parking lot, I explained how she could accept Jesus and find assurance of eternal life. She became frightened as soon as I mentioned Jesus Christ, God's Son. I asked if she would like to pray and give her life to Jesus, but she became very agitated and said that she couldn't pray.

I was outside of the car by then, and I offered her a *Four Spiritual Laws* booklet. I asked her if I could pray for her, but she said no. So I walked the short distance to my plane and set my suitcase down. Then I looked back and noticed her staring first at me and then at my plane. I'm not sure why I did it, but I locked my eyes on hers and started walking back towards her, praying as I went that God would remove the evil one's influence from this woman.

Suddenly she put her car in reverse, squealed the tires, and got out of there as fast as she could. I thought to myself, "How can such an attractive young lady be so far from God?"

On the next leg of the journey, my pastor, who had more experience as a pilot than I did, was flying the plane as we traveled to the Fair Havens Retreat Centre near Orillia. He had asked permission to land on the golf course at the retreat center, which we had done without any problems once before. As we approached the golf course, we encountered unusual levels of turbulence, and he had trouble setting the plane down on the short stretch of grass before us. To compound things, as we touched down we found that the grass was wet, and braking properly was impossible!

My pastor and pilot tried to veer sharply to avoid hitting some bushes, and the front landing gear collapsed. The propeller immediately started churning into the grass, and then we crashed into some trees, coming to a stop very quickly. I had the door open before we crashed, afraid of it jamming and trapping us in the plane. We both jumped out unhurt and quickly moved away from the plane. It was badly damaged, but there was no fire. That evening we had the dubious honor of our plane crash being covered on the Toronto evening news. I can think of better ways to get in the news!

Plane Crash near Orillia, Ontario

I had come to Fair Havens as a delegate to the national convention of the AGC denomination. When I met with the executive secretary, he asked me what had happened. I told him the story of our crash and then also mentioned my experience just thirty to forty minutes earlier with the woman involved in the occult in Guelph. We both came to the conclusion that what I had experienced was an attack by Satan. It was right as the Satan worshiper was staring at me and my plane that a heavy shower suddenly started at the golf course, and the atmosphere there became denser, causing turbulence.

I remembered how Satan had manipulated the elements to attack Job's family (see Job 1:18–19). Reflecting on this, it was difficult to concentrate during the retreat. I was beginning to learn that when we seek first God's kingdom and His righteousness and intentionally seek to be about His business in all that we do, we can expect opposition from the evil one. But God is always there to help, and I sought his help now.

I remembered that Jesus quoted God's Word when He was faced with Satan's temptations in the wilderness, and Satan backed off. When we face our own wilderness experiences, it is often God preparing us for a greater role than we have had in the past. Our trials teach us not to depend on our own strength, but to look to Him for strength in all situations. As we turn to the Lord in the midst of trials and temptations, He shows His power and love, and this gives us confidence in Him as we go into the next role that He has prepared for us.

I could not have imagined the journey of faith that the next two decades would represent for me, far more complex and challenging than anything I had yet faced, but they would also bring an ever increasing sense of God's abiding love. Recognizing that Jesus is the Vine and I am simply a branch helped me to look to God for strength and depend on Him, knowing that I cannot bear fruit otherwise. It also reminded me that if I am going to bear much fruit, which has always been my goal, I have to expect to be pruned. A new chapter of my life was about to begin.

CHAPTER XVI

Back to Millar

"I am the vine; you are the branches. If a man remains in me and I in him, he will bear much fruit; apart from me you can do nothing" (John 15:5).

My relationship with Millar Memorial Bible Institute had begun in 1965 when I was a student there. Shortly after my time at Millar we founded Rem Manufacturing, and we had been very busy building our business and serving the Lord in a variety of ministries in subsequent years. Then, in 1974, I was invited to serve on the board at Millar.

Helen and I prayed about this opportunity to serve the Lord in a new way, and we became convinced that God was leading me back to Millar, this time as a board member. My respect for Mr. Peeler, the principal, was a significant influence on my willingness to serve in this new role. Within a year, though, Mr. Peeler was unable to continue as principal. He had served at Millar for forty years in total, and now due to health problems his future was uncertain.

Millar Memorial Bible Institute had always operated on the basis of trust more than explicit policies. Its culture of unwritten rules had served the school well, and it was operating at capacity in 1974. But around that time, strange teachings began to find their way onto the Millar campus. One teacher began discussing questionable exorcism practices. Others began promoting the "freedom" that Christians have, leading students to indulge their fleshly desires and become worldly. I recall one teacher writing an article that claimed that Jesus did not have to die physically, that it was only a spiritual battle that He had to win. He discussed this theory openly in his classes. As a result of what was going on, many students left and did not return. Some even joined other faith traditions altogether.

The tension was growing among the teaching staff during this period, but it reached a peak when Mr. Peeler was no longer able to give leadership. The board knew it needed to take action, but the members of the board were also old and tired. They began discussing how to replace Mr. Peeler and suggested asking him to move out of the new residence that belonged to the college to make way for whoever the new leader would be. I could not agree with the board on this approach and let them know that it was the wrong decision to try and replace Mr. Peeler. I reminded them that I had myself been a student at Millar and told them that the school was really Peeler Institute, since he had had such an overwhelming role in shaping and running the school. I suggested that we needed to pray for Mr. Peeler's health and trust God to heal him.

Although I had opposed the rest of the board on this issue, the result of my firm stance was that I was soon asked to become chairman of the board. The board members had already prayed, and they all had agreed to ask me.

I, too, needed to pray and seek wisdom from the Lord before making a decision. After prayer, another meeting, and further discussion, I agreed. God had given me a new role, one that I would never have imagined, but that is the life of being a branch connected to the Vine. God directs; we follow.

As chairman of the board, my first order of business was to give assurance to Mr. and Mrs. Peeler that the residence they were living in was theirs to keep. They would have a lifelong lease as part of their benefits for their years of service to the school. We added a dean to handle administrative duties, and Mr. Peeler's job description was changed to just teaching and occasional travel on behalf of the school at his own discretion.

With there being no functional leader, I soon was pressed to take the title of president as well. I called a meeting with the faculty and explained that I couldn't be both chairman of the board and president of the institute.

God had called me to be chairman only. This was acceptable to them, with one exception. They wanted me to take on one function that would be out of the usual description: I was to be responsible for the spiritual tone of the institute. This would include sorting out and dealing with the many divisive issues and personnel problems that had created so much turmoil and resulted in reduced attendance.

What followed were many difficult decisions that had to be made, time-consuming job interviews, and dealing with some difficult people. Some of the older men on the board were now satisfied that the board would move forward, so they felt free to retire. I offered to make them honorary members of the board and invited them to sit in on some of our meetings. We called them "the three wise men."

We hired our first public relations person and formed an executive committee whose job was to plan board meetings and give advice to the chairman of the board. It was crucial that we develop a vision for the long-term. We also hired a campus developer to help plan the future of the campus as we considered relocating some buildings and removing other buildings altogether. We held a public meeting to formalize our many decisions, shifting away from the culture of unwritten rules that had governed life at Millar for many years.

With all the challenges I was facing, I recognized how important prayer support was. Mrs. Peeler became a key prayer supporter, and Gladys Klaasen, a missionary who lived in Swift Current, organized a prayer group for the school. I also started an advisory council that met twice a year and was informed of how to pray for the school. The advisory council became an excellent source for finding new board members. We created a finance committee where we discussed what financial success looked like from a biblical perspective. I found a very important reminder in Proverbs that wisdom is worth more than gold or rubies. I had come to recognize that if we are wise and act by faith, we can trust God to bring the necessary finances.

And this proved to be true; for the next fifteen years we kept on building and improving the campus continuously. But there were always just enough challenges to never let us forget the truth of John 15:5. Jesus is the Vine, and we are merely branches; but as we abide in Him, we are able to bear much fruit!

Thanks to the Lord answering the prayers of many, Mr. Peeler regained his health and accepted a newly defined role as president. He was soon teaching again, with many of the presidential responsibilities delegated to his successor in training. I recall Mr. Peeler commenting around this time that to be a leader at Millar you needed to know how to milk a cow! His point, of course, was that a leader needed to be a servant first and foremost.

"I will praise the LORD, *who counsels me; even at night my heart instructs me"* (Psalm 16:7).

After serving as president for eight years, Mr. Peeler decided to leave that role and concentrate on teaching. His valuable teaching over the years had influenced students to serve as missionaries in forty different countries. Always in demand at conferences, Mr. Peeler was the best speaker around according to Dr. Henry Hildebrandt, former president of Briercrest Bible College. It was quite appropriate when in 1988 Briercrest Bible College awarded Mr. Peeler an honorary doctorate of Christian ministry.

Herbert Peeler receiving an honorary doctorate
from Briercrest College and Seminary, 1988

A NEW WATER SUPPLY

The water supply at the Millar campus had always been inadequate and poor in quality. So around 1980 we decided to attempt to drill down to 1,300 feet and tap the Judith River formation underground. Others in the vicinity had been successful in finding water, but our drilling rig went down as far as 1,400 feet and still found nothing. The conclusion was that the village of Pambrun was sitting on an island of the underground aquifer. One of the locals told me that Pambrun had always been dry. He quipped that even at the time of Noah's flood, Pambrun only got a half inch of rain! But we still needed a solution to our water problems, so we continued praying for God to supply our need.

One day a Mr. Roper called me from the Moose Jaw Prairie Farm Rehabilitation Association (PFRA). He had been working at the PFRA for thirty years and had recently studied the photographs of the air survey in the Pambrun area. He said that it showed surface formations indicating an underground spring four miles west of Pambrun! It appeared that Russell Creek had at one time flowed there and had left a bay area. The land at that location was owned by Norman Fraser, who was willing to help us find good, clean water.

Now that we had found an adequate supply of very good quality drinking water nineteen feet below the surface, how could we bring it to Pambrun? Again we prayed. During that time we were in the middle of a drought, and we soon learned that the government was offering grant money for water projects. We were able to get some assistance from the government and a lot of advice from the PFRA engineer, who told us that the water source was eighty feet higher in elevation than Pambrun. This meant that the pipeline would not need to be pressurized and we could use a smaller diameter pipe. As a result, the project cost about half of the original estimate.

At the dedication ceremony for our new water line, I was asked to share some comments. I focused on the theme of God being the source of wisdom. We needed to thank Him for answering our prayers after many years. After trusting in the Lord and working together as a community, we had achieved success. That well is still pumping in 2013!

Finding a bountiful water supply was a major turning point in our long-range planning for the school. We now knew that we could stay in

Pambrun and continue to grow, rather than having to find a new location for the school.

NEW DEGREE PROGRAMS

If you call out for insight and cry aloud for understanding, and if you look for it as for silver and search for it as for hidden treasure, then you will understand the fear of the LORD and find the knowledge of God (Proverbs 2:3–5).

During my years as chairman of the board we began to seriously consider how Millar could begin granting degrees. We concluded that we would try to offer a four-year program that involved practical ministry experience and would carry degree status: a bachelor of arts in strategic ministry. We were fortunate to have a very astute Christian lawyer volunteer his time to help us find a way to grant a degree.

Provincial law was clear. Only two universities could grant degrees, the University of Saskatchewan and the University of Regina. After much prayer and searching the law, however, our lawyer found that there was one exception to this rule: religious colleges! Millar was now free to begin offering formal degrees, and with this change came a change of name. Millar Memorial Bible Institute became Millar College of the Bible in 1988.

"The joy of the Lord is your strength" (Nehemiah 8:10).

By 1987 I had been serving as chairman of the Millar board for over twelve years, and it was time for a one-year sabbatical from board service. During that year, the recession led to a significant shortage of cash at the college, and leaders responded by taking out a large bank loan. Not only did the loan quickly grow, but they also emptied the school's retirement fund to try to keep the school going. Before my one-year leave was up, a board delegation came to ask me to rejoin the board as chairman.

We needed to be very careful in the difficult circumstances that the college was facing. The board took over the financial management of the college, and the president resigned. We announced an interim president from the faculty team. We realized that the large bank loan needed to be paid off, and Mr. Peeler offered advice regarding who could help us in our need. We offered an ambassador plaque to those willing to help financially in our time of need. After two years of prayer, generous donations, and careful management we had a burning ceremony to celebrate our debt-free status.

In 1991, I left a well-developed board and a college without debt, but my connection to Millar College of the Bible was not over. Helen and I continued to financially support the school. At the turn of the century Mr. Peeler came to see me. He told me that he had never been so concerned about the welfare of Millar College as he was right then, and he asked if I would be willing to help with the board again.

Did God want me to give leadership again, in a time of trouble, with his help?

When I heard these things, I sat down and wept. For some days I mourned and fasted and prayed before the God of heaven. Then I said: "O Lord, God of heaven, the great and awesome God, who keeps his covenant of love with those who love him and obey his commands, let your ear be attentive and your eyes open to hear the prayer your servant is praying before you day and night for your servants" (Nehemiah 1:4–6).

I began to ask how the college was stewarding its resources. I was told that faculty had to find summer jobs elsewhere and that there was an urgent need for more resources. We discovered at that time that the college did not actually officially own the campus property. When the college had been started, the title to the property had been left in the name of the Dickson family, who had farmed there. There were also questions about legal access to the college and the state of the lagoon system. The water supply was not adequate to keep the campus grounds watered. The water line underground was showing signs of aging, with many repairs required. The leadership personnel were gone. The board members were attempting to deal with the local church and their use of campus property. The chapel building was in disrepair, including lack of proper drainage. All of these factors pointed to the urgent need for action.

After several months, I met with the board and found myself thinking that I could not see myself being a member again. And yet I had a strong intuition that I *should* be a board member, even against my better judgment.

I asked to be in charge of gaining title to the lagoon property and after some reluctance was given the job in 2002. When the opening came, I became chairman of the board once again. We immediately began a program to get the college's financial situation back on track.

In an investigation with the Saskatchewan water department we found that Pambrun had the water rights to ten acre-feet of water to use at the discretion of the community. After gaining access to the border property from Mr. Norman Fraser and gaining title to the thirty-acre lagoon property, we donated an earth-moving outfit, scraper, and tractor and constructed a reservoir for the water. While we had the earth mover, we also used it to fill in and level a new soccer field, adding top soil and getting it ready for irrigation.

Another task that was completed at this time was having the college property registered in the name of the college. The staff and faculty would now be employed year-round. We had surveyors define individual lots on the campus, making it possible for staff and faculty to become private property owners with an agreement clause in place. We built a new large shop, which became a landmark.

When we were almost finished building the shop, the walls of the gymnasium started cracking, and we realized that the roof was starting to cave in. The structural engineer condemned the building, allowing no entry except for repair. We discovered that the wooden beams in the ceiling were separating due to inferior glue used to construct them. This needed immediate attention, with the fall term only four months away.

We took the two most qualified men from Rem and began by building screw jacks, seventeen feet high, to raise the roof back to its original height. The repair job was completed in time for the youth retreat, thanks to God's goodness and a lot of hard work.

Finally, be strong in the Lord and in his mighty power. Put on the full armor of God so that you can take your stand against the devil's schemes. For our struggle is not against flesh and blood, but against the rulers, against the authorities, against the powers of this dark world and against the spiritual forces of evil in the heavenly realms (Ephesians 6:10–12)

During my final four years on the Millar board, we encountered a fair bit of opposition. Being a branch connected to the Vine doesn't mean that things will be easy or that things will go smoothly. Being in a battle will leave soldiers with wounds, and we were no exception. But those wounds heal over time and are worth the final outcome. From 2003 to 2007 we watched as both the board and leadership of the college were strengthened. God graciously brought solutions to the financial problems of the school, with a number of individual businessmen stepping up to carry heavy loads in response to the band of prayer warriors who had been faithfully interceding for the school.

My time on the Millar board was now over after twenty years of service between 1974 and 2007. It was time for new challenges. Before we turn to those challenges, though, I need to share what God was doing in our lives in the 1990s and early years of the new millennium as we sought to live as branches connected to the Vine, being about our Father's business one day at a time.

Millar College gets a new sign from Rem, 2003

CHAPTER XVII

The 1990s: New Ministries, New Milestones

The 1990s brought new ministries and some important milestones. When I stepped down from the board at Millar College in 1990 after fifteen years, other ministry opportunities quickly came along.

First I became involved with Campus Crusade's "Power to Change" video distribution ministry. My role made it necessary to work with twelve local churches, develop a committee, and give leadership in financial matters. As always, there were challenges. We expected a large shipment of videos but found out that they would not be shipped until full payment was received. I got on the phone and told the Campus Crusade leadership that if they did not trust us, we should not be serving the Lord together. I said there was no time to waste; they should ship the videos that day and send us the invoice. In the end, they agreed to do as I had suggested. The ministry went forward, and we had genuine revival in the southwest of Saskatchewan. We worked hard at our follow-up ministry and saw lots of fruit.

How can we as human beings show God our love? Without a doubt, we do this first of all by being obedient to Him (John 14:15, 21, 23), but Helen and I felt the need to demonstrate our love for God in another way. In late April of 1995, we started a forty-day fast, eating no solids, and praying. We wanted to get our focus set on loving God, each other, our family, and neighbors. We kept our regular work schedule, which was challenging as we became weaker from losing weight on our diet of only juices and water. We avoided making any significant decisions during those forty days. Instead, we waited on the Lord, declaring our love for Him and our need for Him to direct our future. We sought to grow deeper in our personal relationship with God and have richer fellowship with Him.

That June we received an invitation to join a handful of businessmen gathering together to discuss how they could help fulfill the Great Commission. We traveled to Colorado, where we listened to a world briefing with about 200 leaders. There we were challenged to consider taking on an MPA—million population area. It just so happened that that was approximately the population of the province of Saskatchewan! Helen and I quickly came to believe that God wanted us to take on the commitment of reaching our province with the gospel. That would be our focus for the next seven years—planning a variety of media programs, organizing a telephone program for follow-up, and recruiting and training a team of volunteers. Over the course of our involvement in this program more than 9,000 people indicated a desire to become followers of Jesus Christ. Unfortunately, our follow-up program did not seem to be nearly as successful.

As our giving increased during the 1990s our business prospered. Around 1993, we began to support missionaries who were serving in leadership at the Bibelschule Brake in Germany. We also became more involved in short-term mission trips, including one to the Paz Mission in Santé Ron, Brazil, in the early 1990s.

After our time there was over, the mission asked if I would stay longer and help them with some other projects. I told them that I would be very willing to help but did not have to be there to do it. We worked with a marine engineer to redesign their river boats to help local pastors in their outreach programs. This brought new joy in the Lord and deep excitement about what God was going to do through their ministries.

In August of 1996, Helen and I celebrated our fiftieth anniversary. A half-century together had gone so quickly! They had been busy and eventful years, with many challenges and many triumphs. Best of all, we had walked through them together, trusting God one day at a time for the strength, grace, and resources that we needed.

That October, Helen and I went to Germany and had the privilege of meeting some of Helen's relatives who had recently moved from the Soviet Union. It was a great celebration with her family.

With Helen's relatives in Germany, 1996

Dr. Bill Bright organized prayer and fasting seminars in California in the 1990s, and in November of 1995 I attended one of these with three pastors from Swift Current. This got me thinking about how we could encourage prayer and fasting back home. In early March of 1997, Stuart and I organized a prayer and fasting rally in Swift Current. We were amazed by the response God brought. In the end, 1,300 people attended from all over Saskatchewan. The ultimate size of the rally made it very expensive, and no funds were forthcoming to meet the financial needs we had. In the end, Helen and I committed to underwriting this ministry ourselves, trusting that God would provide as He had always done before.

Less than two weeks after the rally, the spring flood of March 19, 1997 arrived. It was the kind of flood that only happens once every century, and our private bridge at the farm, which was 170 feet long, floated off its foundation! The floodwaters brought huge chunks of ice that carried away much of our irrigation system—pumps, equipment, and the wheel lines of our sprinklers. Although we did not have insurance for these items, God was very good to us through our business, and all of the losses from the flood and our ministry commitments were taken care of.

The flood of 1997 washed away our bridge

As we continued to think about how we could maximize our commitment to the Great Commission, we decided to establish a foundation. We firmly believed that our business belonged to God and was to be used for His glory. We discovered that we could have Rem own some of the company shares and the foundation own the rest. Because the shareholders were few in number, Helen and I agreed to go ahead with the foundation in 1995. Difficulties came, however, when the foundation had funds to give away but Rem Enterprises had a very tight financial cycle. At that point, ministry priorities and business priorities came into conflict. Should we keep on giving to the various ministries we were involved with and allow our accounts with suppliers to go overdue?

One day our banker who managed the credit we depended upon during business cycles, which fluctuated with the seasons, came to see me. He said, "I know your reports are always accurate, and we depend on you for those reports. When you have a commitment to keep in your charitable giving, do you keep giving when there is no surplus and money becomes scarce to pay all bills on time?"

I told him that our giving was based on pledges and depended on our ability to pay. As we prospered, we were able to support various ministries. We did not give money that we did not have.

Our banker was very relieved. He said it helped him to understand our commitment and our dedication. He was very pleased by our approach.

118

My advice to other business owners has always been that integrity has to be a top priority. We must always carry through on any commitments we make, whether the deal is verbal or written. A commitment is a commitment. Our integrity is a foundational component of our character, so we need to ensure total honesty in all circumstances. This is not only pleasing to the Lord but also impacts how others treat us. When our business has needed extra credit, we have always been able to go to those who had confidence in our integrity and knew that we would always be responsible in paying back our loans.

The approach to giving that I shared with our banker, though, did not mean that Helen and I took any of our commitments lightly. We believed that we had to try our utmost to keep our commitments and were ready to make personal sacrifices when our business did not generate the necessary resources. God intervened many times and helped us as we took full responsibility for our pledges, giving by faith and continuing to operate the business that God had entrusted to us.

Eventually we discovered that the foundation was not an essential factor in our charitable giving. The way that the foundation was structured at that time seemed to complicate matters rather than helping. So we decided to eliminate the shares the foundation held in Rem and our farm property. We continued the foundation with a small board of directors, and it became an efficient and valuable method of handling some of our charitable giving.

CHAPTER XVIII

Ministering to the Nations

MEXICO

The leadership team of twenty-six business and professional personnel arrived in Tepic, Mexico, in February of 2001. Tepic is the capital city of the state of Nayarit, located a bit over two hours drive from Puerto Vallarta, with approximately 300,000 residents. There is a fairly large lake about thirty minutes northwest from Tepic. In the middle of the lake, about a twenty-minute boat ride away, is a large island. We were told that this was where the Aztec nation got started.

My team of five set up our equipment on a vacant lot in a residential area, getting everything ready to show the *Jesus* film that evening. But when the time came to start the generator, it wouldn't start. It was getting late, and we were running out of time to show the film. After some effort, we were able to locate a long electrical cord that would reach into a house across the street. Unfortunately, that house turned out to have no power!

Eventually we were able to get permission to plug the cord in at another house. At last we were ready to begin. To our surprise the crowd had grown much larger while we were busily trying to get the generator running.

After the film we gave an altar call, and a man began yelling and crying very loudly. As we gathered around him and began praying, he quickly settled down.

After the meeting was over, we walked to a major street, trying to find transportation back to our hotel. Eventually a taxi came along, but it only had room for four people, and there were five of us. I stayed behind and found myself in a strange place with no ability to speak the language.

Before long, one of the members of the church came along in an old Datsun pickup, and he gave me a ride. Unfortunately, he could not speak English, and my Spanish was limited to *buenos noches* ("good night"). As we wound through side streets and back alleys I got nervous, not being sure of where we were headed, and began to sing Christian songs. Soon the driver joined me in Spanish, and several other voices joined in. I discovered that there were people in the back of the pickup under the cap cover! Somehow, by God's grace, after bumping over potholes and winding all over town, we eventually made it to my hotel.

While we were in the area, our group received an invitation from the local state university for one of us to speak in one of their largest classes. There would be 177 students there. When we realized that they were engineering students, I was given the privilege to lecture. The only limitation that the professor set was that I was not allowed to talk about God or the Bible. I asked him if I could speak on emotional intelligence, and he responded that that would be an excellent topic. When I told him that I would have to talk about the wisdom that comes from God as described in the book of Proverbs, he said that would be fine.

When it was my turn to speak, one of the teachers offered to translate. He just happened to be an evangelical Christian! I began by talking about pneumatic engineering, moving material with air pressure or a vacuum in farm machinery. Then I said, "You clearly have specialized talents. Your high scores in engineering make that clear. You will soon graduate and begin your careers. But specialized talents are not enough to succeed in a manufacturing job. As with much of life, your level of success will largely depend on your ability to get along with others. I want you to think about three questions. First, can you have a debate with others or disagree with others without becoming angry? Second, can you communicate to a group without fear? And third, do you get along well at home with your family?" I shared with them that the wisdom and power we need to be able to answer "yes" to all of these questions comes from God, and they could get to know Him personally, as I had.

Speaking to Engineering class in Tepic, Mexico, 2002

When I opened it up for questions, the first one was "Which God are you talking about?"

I responded, "The Bible tells us that there is only one true God."

This question was quickly followed by another. I couldn't have paid the student to ask a better question: "Do you know this God personally? And how did you get to know Him?"

All of a sudden I was on the very ground the professor had insisted that I avoid. I turned to the translator and said, "I was asked not to talk about religion. What should I say?"

His response was, "They are asking questions, so answer them."

I proceeded to explain how Jesus died and rose again and offers to all who will put their faith in Him the gift of eternal life.

When the professor announced that our time was up and we had to vacate the classroom, one of the students told us, "I'm glad we talked about God and the Bible. I want to get to know God too." We told him to bring his friends and meet us at a service club nearby.

When he arrived, there were fifteen young men with him, and before they left thirteen of them had prayed to accept Jesus. Praise God! He had sent that translator at just the right time. And He used the words of eternal life in a mighty way. There was great rejoicing among the engineering students of the state university in Tepic that day.

It was another beautiful picture of God working through simple branches. We need only to be seeking to honor Him one day at a time.

BENIN

It was 2003, and the drought in Benin, West Africa, was severe. Many were suffering not only from hot temperatures but also from unclean drinking water, the only water they had access to. Word reached Marvin Kehler of Campus Crusade that fresh water wells were desperately needed, and he asked if we would be willing to become involved.

After much prayer we began to familiarize ourselves with the conditions in Benin. Groundwater is plentiful at forty to seventy meters in a large part of the country. There were no roads in most areas, and this was particularly true in the areas of greatest need. Rem Enterprises became involved by designing and building an undercarriage trailer with good suspension so that the drilling rig would have a low center of gravity and could handle the rough roads. It would also carry tool boxes, a generator, a welder, and other necessities.

The engineering and research and development staff also worked many hours to fine-tune the drilling unit before sending it to Africa. The drilling rig was reinforced and carefully designed for simple operation. Native operators were trained by the staff of GAIN (Global Aid Network), and the drilling began. Today there are 100 wells in operation, serving 300 villages.

The redesigned trailer, tool boxes, and well drilling unit for Benin, 2004

HAITI

In 2008, four hurricanes devastated the landscape of Haiti and brought major difficulties to an already very poor and needy people. One of the urgent needs was for drinking water. Some months before the storm, Bob Davisson had informed Helen and me that there was an urgent need for a tanker truck to haul drinking water in his region of Haiti. They had found a very good spring of fresh water, but it was too far from the populated area to build a pipeline. Bob asked if we would be interested in purchasing a 2,000-gallon tanker truck to transport water to the orphanage where Bob worked providing meals and education for children. I asked him to send me a sample of the water to test and found that the quality was very good, requiring minimal treatment. So Helen and I purchased the truck.

Soon after the hurricane disaster came the terrible earthquake of January 2010. Helen and I were filled with joy to realize how God's leading helped to supply vital life-giving water, together with the water of life—the gospel—to the schools for children in Haiti.

ISRAEL

In 2006, I had a wonderful opportunity to visit both Israel and Egypt with a team of four businessmen, a Canadian MP, and the executive director of the Christian Embassy of Canada. It was a great blessing to see the city of Jerusalem, with its ancient walls, and to visit the Mount of Olives, the garden where Jesus prayed on the night before He died for us. The olive trees are still producing 2,000 years later. I picked up a few olives that had fallen to the ground and reflected on what had taken place many years earlier in the place where I was then standing.

Golgotha, the "place of the skull," was very easy to identify with its distinctive rock formations that look very much like skulls. The traditional site of the garden tomb is close by. I wondered, "Could it be possible that this is the location where Jesus—Yeshua—was placed after He died on the cross?" Many years have come and gone, but the new covenant in His blood still stands. The death that Jesus died once and for all is still covering the sins of all those who call upon His name.

"The earth is the LORD's, and everything in it, the world, and all who live in it; for he founded it upon the seas and established it upon the waters" (Psalm 24:1–2).

While we were in Israel we were given an opportunity to sit in the Knesset, Israel's parliament. We were also invited to meet with the executive committee, the ruling cabinet. What a privilege! As we listened to their vision for the future and the tremendous challenges facing the nation of Israel, we were struck by how difficult it is for them to live without fear, given their circumstances. The tension in Israel at that time was severe. Tourists were staying away, some roads were closed altogether, and there had been a recent bombing in the center of Jerusalem, where a new café had been blown up by a terrorist bomb. They had to be constantly vigilant to maintain security.

CAIRO

Teach us to number our days aright, that we may gain a heart of wisdom (Psalm 90:12).

From Israel, we flew to Jordan and then on to Cairo, Egypt, a city of 16 million people. At certain times of the year, with a steady stream of tourists and people traveling there on business, the population can swell to close to 20 million during the daytime hours. We met with people from the commerce department at the Canadian embassy and with a variety of Egyptian business people. They asked us, "Why are you here?"

We told them that we had come to visit those whom we viewed as our neighbors. "We are called to love God and to love our neighbors. We have come to tell you about God's love for you. He sent His Son to die for our sins, and He raised Him from the dead."

Later we visited with a Campus Crusade ministry team on the outskirts of the city. To get back to our hotel required a forty-minute ride on a six-lane highway. Our taxi was a small vehicle that was about twenty years old. It was very crowded with four passengers and the driver. All of the windows were down, and soon the traffic fumes were pouring in.

Our translator was sitting in the back seat with my companions, while I was in the front beside the driver. I thought it would be better with the windows up, but when I went to roll up my window there was no way to do it. I asked the driver if we could close the windows, and he handed me a crank that did not have a knob. I put the crank in place and proceeded to close my window. After that, he closed his partway. I guess he had come to prefer having some ventilation, even if it was polluted air pouring in the window.

The interpreter told me that if I wanted to talk with the driver he would translate. I prayed and then asked him, "Do you love God?"

He quickly responded, "No."

I then told him, "Well, God loves you."

This time he gave a fuller answer: "That's impossible. Nobody loves me."

I went on to explain to him, "God sent His Son to die for you, showing how much He loves you."

The taxi driver began to explain his problems to me, and I shared with him how God had the answer to his problems. I told him that God had a plan for his life as well as mine, and I explained how he could receive the gift of salvation if he sought forgiveness from God and pledged his allegiance to Him.

The taxi driver said that if God could love him, someday he might accept Him. I reminded him, though, that his life was very uncertain. "Every day there are accidents in these busy streets. What if you should die tonight without knowing the way to heaven?" After that, we were quiet until we came to our hotel.

When we stopped in front of the hotel, as I climbed out of the cab I looked at the taxi driver and said, "You are free to go now, but if you want to stay, I will help you become a believer and a follower of Jesus." The taxi driver said he wanted to pray. I asked if he would be willing to meet the next day with the translator so that he could explain more fully what it means to pledge our allegiance to the Lord, to make God the Lord of our life. He said the he would gladly meet with the translator. We prayed for him, and he prayed the sinner's prayer. As he drove off into the Cairo traffic that night, he went with a broad smile on his face. All praise to our God, who seeks out and saves the lost, including a taxi driver in Cairo who felt totally unloved.

My fellow travelers from Canada were amazed at the total change in the driver's attitude over the course of little more than half an hour. They had never witnessed this before. Once again I was reminded of Jesus' words: "I am the vine; you are the branches. If a man remains in me and I in him, he will bear much fruit" (John 15:5). Sometimes the "remaining" is as simple as watching for the opportunities for us to bear fruit that God brings. God had prepared the heart of the taxi driver. He had planned for us to meet him. All we had to do was open our mouths and share the Good News. He brought the fruit.

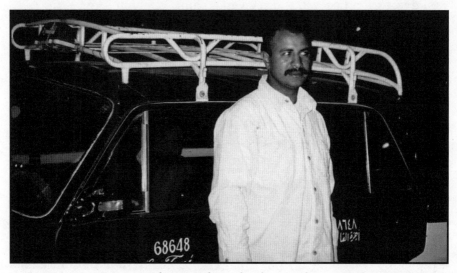

Cairo taxi driver and new brother in Christ, 2006

Perhaps the only reason God sent me to Cairo was so that I could ride in that taxi and talk to that man who needed to hear of God's love for him so that he could be saved. What other opportunities might He still have in store for me, or for you?

OTTAWA

"How beautiful are the feet of those who bring good news!" (Romans 10:15).

It was 2004, and I had come to Ottawa to do a presentation on Rem at an ambassador luncheon sponsored by the Christian Embassy ministry. I was told that I would also have time to share my faith. There were thirty-four countries represented by their ambassadors and their staffs. Some members of the Canadian parliament were also there. Our grandson Mike had helped me prepare a PowerPoint presentation.

Mike handled the computer and kept the slides coming as I shared the story of Rem. I showed pictures of many of our products and shared how I had come to know God personally. I told them how knowing God had impacted our business and that God had intervened for us time and time again as we had chosen to follow Him.

As part of the presentation, I told them about our humanitarian project in Benin and showed a picture of the Rem well drilling machine that we had donated. The ambassador of Benin was there, and this was the first time he had heard that we had been in his country. He was very pleased, and we quickly became friends. I concluded my presentation with John 14:6 ("Jesus answered, 'I am the way and the truth and the life. No one comes to the Father except through me'") and a prayer for all of them.

Sometime later the ambassador of Benin told me a story. "I was invited to Saskatchewan by the premier, and he asked me what I knew about Saskatchewan." The ambassador told the premier that they were in Saskatchewan for the first time and all they knew was that there was a company there, in Swift Current, called Rem Enterprises, which had donated a water well drilling machine to his country. He asked the premier if he knew this company called Rem, and the premier said he didn't.

On that trip the ambassador gave us a message from the president of Benin and his wife. The president's wife asked if we would also bring the water-of-life message to the residents of Benin. Ministry teams were sent to each location when the newly drilled wells were beginning to pump water. The *Jesus* film was used to tell about Jesus and the way to eternal life. The villagers were very thankful and responded in great numbers. New churches were built, the first churches in those villages.

Today there are over thirty new churches, and for the first time ever there is fresh, healthy drinking water. Those living in villages with a new well are for the first time open and responsive to the Good News of Jesus Christ. The water well drilling machine called Rem FR is still drilling wells today.

"But from everlasting to everlasting the LORD's love is with those who fear him" (Psalm 103:17).

One of the other ambassadors that day in Ottawa was from Indonesia. His name was Eki, and he later came to stay in our house on a Christian

Embassy sponsored tour in Swift Current. He approached me after the Ottawa meeting and said, "When you're ready, I have my limousine waiting. I want to give you a tour." The limousine was a Mercedes, and the first stop was the residence of the ambassador and his family. They served a freshly cooked Indonesian lunch and talked about their country.

Eki said he would be returning home to Indonesia soon and would be running for political office. He asked if I would come to visit him. I told him I would make plans to do so. He graciously took us to the airport for our flight home, and along the way I asked him, "If we are not able to meet again, will I see you in heaven?"

He told me that the teaching about the Good Shepherd had helped him to understand in a new way the teachings of Jesus. When we reached the airport, he helped me by carrying one of our suitcases. When the two of us were alone, he said, "In answer to your question, I will see you in heaven. I have come to believe." Just a few months later, Eki died of a heart attack in Indonesia, but as far as I know he died as a follower of Jesus.

QUITO
Teach me to do your will, for you are my God; may your good Spirit lead me on level ground (Psalm 143:10).

In 2002, Roy LeTourneau came to Swift Current to speak at a CBMC event (Christian Business Men's Committee), and I asked Roy if he would speak at an outreach meeting at Rem as well. We invited all the employees to come during work hours. They could choose to keep working or come and listen; they would be paid the same either way.

Roy and I became friends, and we talked about many things. At a later meeting together we made plans to build earthmover scrapers like his father, R. G. LeTourneau, had done in the previous generation. Our new scrapers could be pulled by a four-wheel-drive farm tractor with a ball hitch. We also designed a tandem set of scrapers, one behind the first one. But not long after we began to market these scrapers, the price of steel doubled, and then tripled! The Canadian dollar also began to rise in value steadily. As a result, there was no way that we could be competitive with foreign companies, and so we were forced to discontinue the land scraper product.

"My eyes stay open through the watches of the night, that I may meditate on your promises" (Psalm 119:148).

Despite this setback, our friendship was strong. One day Roy asked if I would go to Quito, Ecuador, with him. The LeTourneau foundation had begun a church plant operation called Christian Ministry International. Roy was helping with a program called the Quito Initiative.

Two of us from Canada and four from the USA went to visit. The elevation in Quito is 9,500 feet, and we all noticed a considerable lack of energy as we visited many sites in the area. We were also invited to the revival meetings in the Alliance churches. The highlight, though, was visiting the new church plant.

The church was located in a place that an early missionary had named Cumbayá ("Come by here"). There were new converts meeting in an underground parking area beneath an office tower. Many of these converts were government employees, and some were politicians. They were eager to purchase their own property but were not able to get a bank loan for the US$500,000 that was needed. They asked us if we would be willing to help. After praying and asking the Lord to direct us, Helen and I decided to supply the down payment on the new lot. Today, the first phase of the building, which seats 600 people, has been completed. Every time they gather for worship the building is full!

Mission trip to Quito, Ecuador with the LeTourneau Foundation.

While we were in Quito, we were invited to speak at a men's breakfast where businessmen gathered to hear about Canada and the USA. They asked me, through a translator, "What made you decide to come to visit us in Quito?"

I told them that in the Bible Jesus said that the greatest commandment is to love the Lord your God with all your heart, with all your mind, with all your soul, and with all your strength. I was learning to love God more and more as time went by. He is my Savior and my Lord, and I had decided to follow Him wherever He leads me.

I went on to tell them that Jesus said that the second greatest commandment is to love our neighbors as ourselves, and I had come to Quito because they are my neighbors. We had come to see how we could serve them and to tell them about God's love for them and what He had done for them through His Son Jesus Christ. I quoted from the hymn "The Love of God" in closing:

> Could we with ink the ocean fill
> And were the skies of parchment made
> Were every stalk on earth a quill
> And every man a scribe by trade
> To write the love of God above
> Would drain the ocean dry
> Nor could the scroll contain the whole
> Though stretched from sky to sky.
> (Frederick M. Lehman, 1917)

KENYA

O God, you are my God, earnestly I seek you; my soul thirsts for you, my body longs for you, in a dry and weary land where there is no water (Psalm 63:1).

The Turkana region of northern Kenya is not an easy place to live in. Even in the best of circumstances, life is quite tenuous in this hot and impoverished region of the country.

In 2007, northern Kenya was facing a severe drought once again. The rivers had dried up throughout the region, and the locals were having to dig ever deeper into the riverbed to get their drinking water. The soil—mostly sand—would sometimes cave in and bury alive those who were trying to locate precious water. The buried bodies would then contaminate the well that they had tried to dig.

The heat was almost unbearable, soaring well over 40 degrees Celsius. Thirst, hunger, suffering, and death were the common lot of the locals, with only one out of every five children surviving to the age of five. Most slept outdoors on mats and lived largely on goats' milk, when it was available. They had huts, but they were mainly used when there was excessive wind or dust and during the far too infrequent rainstorms.

A local evangelist and missionary, Pastor Wilson, had asked for our help in his area near the city of Kakuma. And so Stuart and I traveled there in June of 2007. Our goal was to dig a number of wells in the area. We were able to locate a renovated cable-type drilling machine in Nairobi, along with a truck-tractor to pull it the 590 miles north to the Turkana region. Dave McElhinney, a carpenter and missionary from Medicine Hat, Alberta, had arrived a week or so before us, loaded up the drill rig, and headed north. The best speed he was able to maintain was fifty kilometers per hour. More typically he lumbered along at twenty kilometers per hour or less. It was a long trip, with roads washed out, bridges out, and plenty of detours, but we eventually arrived in Kakuma.

The destination for the first well was thirty kilometers from Kakuma. The people there had to walk five miles every day to get water, which was poor in quality. On our first trip to this village, in a Range Rover, we were met by a group of men carrying spears and shields. It was an apparent show of force, with them still being uncertain of exactly what our intentions were. We did a lot of handshaking and made careful note of the layout of their huts and location of their goats.

Transporting the drilling rig the thirty kilometers from Kakuma required a day and a half of careful travel navigating the washouts, road construction, and paths that could hardly be called roads. When we arrived we hired a native crew to run the drill, and Dave began training them.

At last the rig started drilling the well, and our first attempt was a resounding success. The well was constructed with a concrete base and a protective fence and was simple enough to operate that young boys would be quite capable of pumping fresh water for drinking and for watering the goats. It produced good, clean water.

Drilling a water well in the Turkana region of Kenya, 2007

When construction was complete, a ministry team gathered to celebrate the new well. The locals were delighted with this new access to water, and their hearts were eager to listen to the message. That day many decisions were made to follow the Lord. The pump quickly became the center of activity for the area, a gathering place for getting the precious commodity of abundant, clean, good-tasting water.

The local witch doctor, however, was very concerned, since he was already losing business thanks to these foreigners and the well they had brought. So he decided to sacrifice an animal to curse the people who had brought the well and curse their ministry as well. Before he could carry out the cursing ceremony, however, a local government policeman who was in the area put a stop to it.

As he considered the new followers of Jesus, Pastor Wilson was concerned for their physical as well as their spiritual well-being. "We need to teach these new converts how to live healthy lives and help them to understand why so many children die so young. We need to provide basic medical help," he told us. Thankfully, the city council in Kakuma was willing to help. They agreed to sell us a ten-acre plot of land at the edge of the city—an ideal spot. The initial price, however, was far too high. We didn't see how purchasing the land was going to be possible, but we continued to pray and trust that the Lord would show us His plan.

Our time there was quickly coming to an end, and it looked like purchasing the land was not going to happen. In God's sovereign plan, though, Stuart and I ended up being detained there for an extra day. We were pleasantly surprised when the city leaders came to us and said, "We will let you have this plot of land for less than ten percent of its value if you pay cash now." Perhaps God did want us to go forward with the land purchase.

When we asked Wilson how much money he had on hand, though, he replied quite simply, "Nothing."

We were left asking, "What should we do?"

Stuart and I had brought enough American cash to go on a safari while we were in Kenya. As we considered the city leaders' offer, we counted up our money and found that we had enough to purchase the land, with $100 left over. We quickly made the decision and paid for the land, but that was only the beginning.

It took a full eighteen months for us to receive the title to the land. At that point we were free to build a fence and drill for water, but this time we encountered a dry hole. It took another eighteen months before we could get access to a large drilling machine that could drill through the rock that seemed to permeate the land we had purchased. This time we located fresh, clean water—four years after we purchased the land.

During the time in Kenya when Stuart and I were delayed, we also had an opportunity to help a missionary who had become very ill with a flu. We found medication and contacted a doctor who was 500 miles away to get advice. We were also able to rent an air-conditioned hut to bring the missionary some relief from the soaring temperatures.

The next day, though, both Stuart and I became ill with the same flu! We arrived home suffering from the strange illness, and a month later I developed a heart condition that left me with angina and shortness of breath.

After six months of these symptoms, I called three pastors from the Alliance church, one of whom had just come home from the Philippines, Dr. Bob Kuglin. Together they anointed me with oil and offered a prayer of faith, and God instantly healed my heart. To this day, five years later, my heart is healthy and strong. Praise God!

The well drilling project in the Turkana region continues today. The drilling team typically has to go forty to seventy meters down in order to locate water, and frequently there is no water to be found. In such cases, the team has to obtain a new drilling permit to try another spot. Progress is slow, but to this point we have been able to drill twenty-four wells.

In 2012 we faced many difficulties with the Kenya ministry. However, we thank the Lord that the men working on the drilling crew have now all become believers and are active in the outreach programs that accompany all of the wells that are drilled.

CHAPTER XIX

Rem: All These Things Shall Be Added Unto You

Many, O LORD my God, are the wonders you have done. The things you planned for us no one can recount to you; were I to speak and tell of them, they would be too many to declare (Psalm 40:5).

As I think back over the years, I cannot help but be struck by the incredible faithfulness of God. He clearly directed Helen and me to start our business, but He didn't stop there. We found time and time again that He really means what He says in Matthew 6:25–34. We really need not worry about how we will make ends meet; God has those details of life all under control. He is a loving Father who is more than capable of taking care of His children. Our role is to be careful to "seek first his kingdom and his righteousness." When we live that kind of God-focused life, God promises to take care of all of our needs.

As I reflect back on what God has done at Rem as we have committed ourselves to honoring Him one day at a time, I am struck by the clear evidence that Rem is not a company that we built by our own blood, sweat, and tears. Nor is it a company that we built by our own ingenuity. Yes, we worked very hard and made many sacrifices, but so do countless others who never see the results that we saw. The fruit that we have seen in both business and ministry has come from the Vine to which we have been connected. He has brought all of the good we have seen in this life, and to Him alone belongs all the glory.

Particularly as we think about the products that really put Rem on the map, we can look back and see that God was directing our path. In the early 1970s, Rem introduced a straw chopper that could both cut and blow straw. It would also save the chopped straw if desired, guiding it and then blowing it into a wagon pulled behind a combine. As news of this new product spread and demand began to increase, a company in Nebraska asked if the chopper could be used with corn husks and corn straw. Their idea was to run the waste material from the corn harvest through the chopper and then use it for cattle feed. This represented new territory for our business, both in terms of geography and the use of our products. I decided to make the trip alone. I would take along the chopper, install it, and test it myself.

The small town I traveled to, near Fairfield, Nebraska, had a service station with Bowser pumps. A hand-operated pump was used to pump the gasoline into a glass container. The fuel then drained from the glass container by gravity—no electricity needed. The streets were paved with tile and had swales for drainage. A room in the local hotel cost two dollars a night, and the bed was something like a hammock with an old mattress in it. The second night I slept in the truck cab, which turned out to be quite a bit more comfortable!

When I went to visit the customer, a young farmer, I found that he had a very modern cattle operation with two new steel silos. Without any physical work he could feed 300 cattle. "I want to make silage out of my corn husks and corn straw. So I need them chopped," he explained. "I also want to be able to move the husks into a John Deere chuck wagon pulled behind the 105 John Deere combine. Can you do it?"

I replied, "My boss thinks it will work," not wanting him to know that I was actually the owner of Rem.

I worked hard all that day and got the chopper installed. While I was working, a neighbor came along. He was wearing a hat like a hillbilly and chewing tobacco. He had nothing positive to say about what I was doing. "What makes you think you can keep the chopper from destroying itself when John Deere can't do it?" he asked. I told him that John Deere had not yet learned how to do it, but we had! I stayed long enough to test run the chopper lower unit, and it worked very well.

After returning home, I didn't hear a word from the farmer. So after the harvest I decided it was time to check in with him. I wanted to see what could be done to plan for improvements for the next year. The farmer told me that the chopper was working just fine. It handled all his corn without any trouble, and when his neighbor saw what it did, he had asked the farmer to help him make feed for his cattle as well. Great news!

I asked him if there were any improvements that might make his work easier or more productive the following year. He replied, "Well, the wagon is quite long and it would be nice if it could blow a little farther, so that I can carry a bigger payload." So I sent him bigger blowers.

This story illustrates the way that the Lord regularly intervened on our behalf, not only giving me ideas for new products, but also directing us into new markets for those products and somehow always making them work well. It all seems quite miraculous as we look back! As we were seeking first His kingdom and His righteousness, He was busy taking care of the details of making the business grow and prosper.

God's guiding hand was very evident in another key event around the same time. A customer from Alberta decided to buy several of our best blowers, but I discovered that the task he intended to use them for required an even more efficient vacuum blower. He had tried himself to develop a cleanup vac but after much effort and illness had finally given up. He decided to sell his ideas to me.

After extensive testing and improvements, we began to market our new product, the 552 GrainVac, in 1985. God had used circumstances, in this case the need of a particular Albertan farmer, to lead us to develop a product that would help define the company. Our GrainVac quickly grew in popularity and is the largest and most popular farm grain vac in the world today.

People are sometimes astounded at what the GrainVacs can do, particularly in the case of our 3700 GrainVac, which can handle 10,000 bushels per hour. One day, one of our customers was talking to the local ethanol plant manager and told him, "I filled a 1,000-bushel corn truck in less than six minutes."

The local ethanol plant manager asked how he had done it, and he said he used a Rem GrainVac. "Impossible!" the agent exclaimed. "There is no grain vac in the world that can do that." The farmer was happy to invite the man to his farm for a demonstration.

"I know that you can do all things; no plan of yours can be thwarted" (Job 42:2).

In the 1980s and 1990s, the product line at Rem kept on growing. The chaff blower had been redesigned to fit the much larger combines that had recently come on the market in our region. We had a new, much improved dump wagon, which was pulled behind the combine. The vacuum feed blower was a new design that would pick up chaff piles left by the dump wagon and blow the chaff into a wagon to haul it away. This invention immediately increased our business substantially. The variety of harrow tines we produced also increased, and we had many new customers.

God continued to bring new ideas and open up new opportunities as we continued to seek first His kingdom and His righteousness. With all the new products, though, we quickly became overcrowded at our plant and began dreaming about a new location with more space to run the business.

As we dreamed and planned for the future, God brought yet another new product to our attention: springs. There was a significant market for extension and compression springs, as well as torsion springs, for the agricultural manufacturing industry. We had heard about the world's largest automatic spring coiler, which was made in Germany and seemed ideal for what we had in mind. So in 1980 off I went to Reutlingen, Germany, where I purchased a Wafios coiling machine, with all the latest upgrades.

World's largest automatic spring coiler, Germany, 1981

Back home in Swift Current, we had become friends with a German immigrant. He had asked that if we ever went to Germany we would go see his friend and help him find assurance of eternal life, just as we had helped him and his wife. So while in Germany I had the privilege of staying overnight with Fritz Resle and his wife in Hilden and sharing with them what Helen and I had learned about the Spirit-filled life. Once again we were amazed at how our work at Rem beautifully dovetailed with the Great Commission God has entrusted to all of His people.

"On my bed I remember you; I think of you through the watches of the night. Because you are my help, I sing in the shadow of your wings. My soul clings to you; your right hand upholds me" (Psalm 63:6–8).

In February of 1981, we began to manufacture at the new location in McIntyre Industrial Park. We were moving from a site with 7,000 square feet to one with 30,000 square feet. It was a huge expansion, but the new equipment we were now using, including the automatic spring coiler, was very large and required far more space than we had needed before. To keep production on schedule we had to continue operating the old plant while we fine-tuned new machinery and brought the new shop up to speed. It was a busy time as we oversaw a larger group of employees.

Rem's new shop in the Highway Industrial Park, Swift Current, 1981

141

We worked very hard in those years, both Helen and I, as well as our son Stuart, who had come to help. We were grateful to the Lord in 1982 as we began to receive significant orders for the new springs we were producing.

"Do not let this Book of the Law depart from your mouth; meditate on it day and night, so that you may be careful to do everything written in it. Then you will be prosperous and successful. Have I not commanded you? Be strong and courageous. Do not be terrified; do not be discouraged, for the LORD your God will be with you wherever you go" (Joshua 1:8–9).

As the business grew, we continued to ask ourselves what it looked like to run it as our Father's business. He had directed us to start the business. We were grateful for the resources the business provided for investing in God's work at home and abroad, but we also wanted to be careful to run the business in a way that would honor God and keep the Great Commission in focus. That meant that we had a responsibility not only to the lost "out there" but also to those working at Rem. We saw this ministry at Rem as a significant part of seeking first His kingdom.

We now had around 100 employees, many of whom were very resistant to anything religious. We had continued to have outreach meetings at Rem on a regular basis (usually two each year). Now some employees began to strongly criticize these meetings. We even began receiving threats: "Stop the religious activity or we will report you!" We knew that we were living in a society that puts strong pressure on Christians to not "impose" their beliefs on others, but we also remembered the words of Peter when he was facing similar pressures: "We must obey God rather than men!" (Acts 5:29). God had commanded us to make disciples, and we needed to be faithful to His commands, regardless of what people around us were saying.

As the leader of Rem I had to take responsibility, and my decision was that we would not change. We would continue to have outreach events and to do our leadership training at Rem based on biblical principles, which emphasized the need for all of us to know God personally. If that meant going to jail, I would go to jail. I told those who opposed me, "You can stop criticizing what we're doing and change your ways, or, if you're not happy here, you can leave. The world is a big place. You're not going to change how this company is run, and we will get by just fine without you." I demonstrated this by dropping a penny in a glass of water. There was a little splash, and then the water was quickly back to normal. No one is indispensable.

"Find rest, O my soul, in God alone; my hope comes from him. He alone is my rock and my salvation; he is my fortress, I will not be shaken. My salvation and my honor depend on God; he is my mighty rock, my refuge" (Psalm 62:5–7).

During this period, I set my mind on improving our charter of values. I saw that with the increase in the size of our workforce we had not adequately communicated our values to our employees. We had not defined our expectations clearly, and so there was not a clear sense of culture. Everyone needed to understand that the company was a family business that was run on biblical values and the morality and integrity that the New Testament calls all followers of Jesus to embrace. So I began putting much more emphasis on character building, particularly with our management team.

This, though, led to five managers leaving in a short interval of time. We lost valuable leaders in accounting and sales. Following Jesus does not mean that things will always go smoothly. Our choices to continue to ensure that Rem was operated as our Father's business had a cost. We had to train new managers, but God brought the right people, and we survived the many challenges in that period. Even when interest rates spiked from 7 percent to more than 20 percent, the farm economy went into recession, and our orders plummeted, God was faithful to see us through.

As the new century approached, our markets continued to expand. Rem was privileged to become an ISO (International Standards Organization), registered in the areas of engineering, production, and marketing. For more than thirty years Rem continued to develop and improve the technology of Rem blowers, and they came to be used very widely in the agricultural industry. We were now a global supplier of pneumatic air blowers for both pressure and vacuum applications. We were also supplying the John Deere Company with blowers for air seeders, drills, and other machinery.

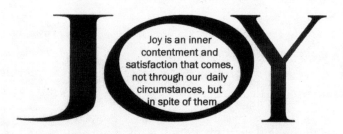

JOY

Joy is an inner contentment and satisfaction that comes, not through our daily circumstances, but in spite of them.

INTEGRITY

We are committed to corporate and personal integrity every day, through every transaction, in every relationship.

Integrity is the quality or condition of being whole, undivided or complete. Integrity means that what we say and what we do are the same.

CHARACTER

Character consists of the qualities or virtues that distinguish us from others. Respect for each other means to regard one another as better than ourselves. Challenging each other means to urge each other on to higher levels of performance.

We respect and challenge each other, and encourage one another to grow in character.

HONOUR

We strive to honour the Lord God by being diligent stewards of the company's resources: people, facilities, money and time.

Honouring the Lord through diligence recognizes that our existence on earth is finite. We do not own anything, but have been merely given resources in trust for the future by Him.

Rem's Values

144

CHAPTER XX

A Decade of Adventure, Discipline, and Growth

For you, O God, tested us; you refined us like silver...we went through fire and water, but you brought us to a place of abundance...Come and listen, all you who fear God; let me tell you what he has done for me. I cried out to him with my mouth; his praise was on my tongue. If I had cherished sin in my heart, the Lord would not have listened; but God has surely listened and heard my voice in prayer. Praise be to God, who has not rejected my prayer or withheld his love from me! (Psalm 66:10, 12, 16–20)

We are very grateful for all that God has done in our lives and for the way that He allowed us to build a family business that He has used to bless many people and fund many wonderful ministries. It was not always clear, though, that Rem would survive. In fact, as a business we faced a full decade of serious testing during which our survival was often in doubt.

Some of our children played significant roles in our business during the latter half of the 1970s. Connie helped us learn to market some of our specialty products, not only in Canada but in many other parts of the world as well. She was always willing to help wherever I needed her, and I was delighted to have her working at my side as my assistant. I was very thankful when Stuart joined us at Rem in the spring of 1976, after finishing a degree in business administration and economics at Bethel College (now Bethel University) in Minneapolis and moving to Waldeck, Saskatchewan, with Joellen and their first daughter, Jody. He not only took over general management of the plant but also helped us to expand our approach to marketing in important ways. This freed me up to spend more time on the actual marketing and sales of our products. All of this led to steady growth in our business.

As we entered the 1980s, business was booming, and we had recently moved to a new location where we had room to continue growing. The consistent growth during the 1970s and early 1980s, though, was not the full story. God had indeed been very good to us and supplied all of our needs as He had promised, but His provision did not always come in the way we expected or according to what we thought would be an appropriate delivery schedule. When we broke ground for our new building in the McIntyre Industrial Park in 1980, the outlook for the Saskatchewan economy, particularly in manufacturing, was very positive. What we did not anticipate was that we would soon face the worst economic conditions in fifty years as we entered into the recession of the 1980s. Although there had been no obvious signals of an impending slowdown in our own sales, with the benefit of hindsight it's obvious that the timing of our massive expansion could not have been worse.

In his book *Yellow Steel: The Story of the Earthmoving Equipment Industry,* William Haycraft notes that by midsummer of 1980 it was clear that what would become a global slowdown was underway in the U.S., with the farm economy leading the way. After more than 150 years in business, and many years of losing money, Harvester (for many years the biggest farm equipment company in the U.S.) was sold in 1984. Similarly, after absorbing other companies with illustrious histories but recent struggles (Oliver, Cockshutt, and Minneapolis Moline), the White Motor Company petitioned for bankruptcy in 1980. The Letourneau Earthmoving business, taken over by Westinghouse some time before, also failed in the early 1980s. Indeed, many more large U. S. firms went defunct, and those that survived, such as Caterpillar, did not do well in agricultural machinery sales during this period. Unfortunately, the same trend held true in Western Canada during the early 1980s, and many farm equipment manufacturing companies failed to survive.

Up until 1980, Rem's debt level had been very low. The expansion, however, changed that dramatically. Not only did we have to cope with financing the new building, we also had a significant increase in our tax burden. Stuart and I put a great amount of time and energy into obtaining a federal grant to assist us. Thus, when the provincial government informed us that the PST (provincial sales tax) for our expansion would be $80,000, we were grateful to God that we ultimately qualified for a federal grant of $75,000 to cover most of it. The Saskatchewan government would later cease to charge PST for industry expansion, but in the early 1980s we felt the burden heavily.

Rem had moved into the new building at the end of December 1980. In January we jumped from fifteen to forty-two employees to accommodate our orders in the spring division and product division. It was the spring division that provided the cash flow for the company. Unfortunately, at the end of February the manufacturing industry screeched to a sudden halt, and all manufacturing companies placed a hold on their spring orders, bringing Rem's business to a halt as well. We slowed down production to a minimum level and limped along for about four or five months, showing losses each month. When we delivered financial statements to our banks in January, they showed a huge loss for the fiscal year.

What really hit us hard during the recession, which we were just entering, were the high interest rates. At a time when we heavily relied on a line of credit, we found interest rates skyrocketing to around 20 percent. To compound things, several of our largest and most important customers, to whom we had sold large amounts of our products on credit, declared bankruptcy. When they failed to recover, we suffered huge losses. Many smaller companies also failed, making our losses even greater. When these companies were unable to pay us, we were left in a position where we could not pay our own suppliers. Although it went against everything we believed in and the values we had built our business on, we were forced to ask them to give us more time to pay our bills. Things were looking very bleak.

We also faced significant stress from our creditors during this period. In fact, the constant concerns expressed by our bankers brought almost daily tension to our lives, and we spent a huge amount of time trying to reassure them. Stuart and I worked furiously, trying to improve our cash flow, taking on major custom work in an effort to pay our bills, and trying to find a way forward for Rem. It was backbreaking work, and we consistently lived on the edge of burnout during those months. I still remember a Christian lawyer friend advising me, "Let it go. It's not worth the severe tensions." He was certainly not exaggerating the pressures we were facing.

Our bankers were not only hounding us regarding what we owed them; they were also trying to convince us to go into bankruptcy. As Stuart and I worked hard to find a way through our financial challenges, our bankers were quick to remind us that no business ever handled its own affairs in this situation. Their suggestion, of course, was that they would send a manager to run the company for us while we went through bankruptcy proceedings. I remember five bankers sitting in my office one day and talking about lowering our line of credit—just when we needed it the most—in an effort to pressure us to go along with their plan. I knew, though, that their plan would only make matters worse. "Your manager will be looking after your interests but will not understand how to manage a high risk family enterprise," I told them. I also reminded them that they had tried this approach with other struggling businesses, and it had failed. Part of my concern was that there would be significant costs in hiring accountants and lawyers in a bankruptcy, and I believed that it was wrong for the business to have to pay for such unnecessary expenses. So I told them firmly, "If you send your man here, I'll hold the door open while my two heavy duty staff throw him out. And he won't be coming back in!" The bankers were very quiet as they left my office and never made another attempt to send their man to manage our company.

This, of course, did not solve our problems. In early March of 1982 the bankers sat down with us, told us that we were no longer liquid, and informed us that they intended to call in their loan. We insisted that this would be a foolish move, since our order backlog was strong and we were back to making profits. We pointed out that all parties would lose if the banks proceeded with their plan. We asked the banks if there was anything we could do to assure them that we were still a viable company. They simply responded with a letter calling in our loans. They agreed to allow us to carry on manufacturing until an independent consultant's report was filed, but because of the call on our loans we would be unable to pay off our suppliers, and we would be forced to pay cash for any future products we purchased from them.

When the consultant's report was submitted, it confirmed that Rem Manufacturing remained a viable company. The banks, however, were still reluctant to withdraw their call on our loans. Eventually, they determined that we needed additional equity to carry on.

I remember coming home one day in 1983 and telling Helen, "We're broke. Let's pray to our Heavenly Father about what to do next." As we were praying, we were both encouraged not to give up. We remembered that "the righteous will live by faith" (Romans 1:17), but we were not sure what that would look like in our current crisis. We were confident that the recession would soon be over and orders would begin coming in again, but we needed a plan for surviving until the economy recovered.

First, I asked my good friend and former employer Jack Carter if he would consider loaning us some money. He agreed without hesitation, and when I received a check for $175,000, Helen and I thanked God for the answer to prayer and the temporary relief we now enjoyed. Then, some of our customers began telling us, "We need some of your products, and we will pay cash in advance." Terry Sumac of Flexicoil in Saskatoon was a major help in this way. Between the loan and the inflow from cash sales, we were able to continue purchasing products from our suppliers using cash, but we were still unable to pay past due invoices, and we still needed to raise new equity.

Stuart played a critical role during this period. He was the one who communicated with our suppliers on a regular basis. He made sure to never miss giving them an update, always telling them exactly how things were going at Rem and letting them know what they could expect. He took great care not to mislead them in any way, and the many years of good relationships we had cultivated with our suppliers helped them to trust us during this difficult time.

Equally important, Stuart and I began planning how we could restructure the company and raise equity. We ultimately decided to take on new shareholders. Stuart would hold 12.5 percent of the company's shares, Helen and I would hold 37.5 percent, and a select group of ten others would together own 50 percent. That sounded like a good plan, but who would want to buy shares, given our financial status, which we made no attempt to hide or sugarcoat?

In addition to finding new equity, our banks were requiring us to go through an informal restructuring proposal with our creditors, offering them thirty-four cents on the dollar. We hoped that if our suppliers agreed to this arrangement, this would provide the incentive the employees, friends, and local businessmen we were inviting to join us as shareholders needed to invest in Rem. Perhaps this plan that Stuart and I had worked so hard to put together would allow our company to weather the economic storms that had caused the demise of so many other manufacturing companies in North America in recent years.

While we were raising the equity and preparing the informal proposal, one of our banks (the Saskatchewan government) entertained a hostile takeover bid from one of our spring manufacturing competitors in Ontario. The competitor was offering our suppliers twenty cents on the dollar. Our suppliers, though, recognized that the Ontario competitor would likely shut down the product division and only maintain the spring division. This would mean that any future business with Rem would be severely limited. As a result, several of them began connecting with other suppliers in an attempt to prevent the hostile takeover. Through their combined efforts they influenced the government bank to decline the offer.

That was not the end of outside pressures on us, however. Twice during the year-long "call" on our loans, a government bank representative called Stuart at home on a Saturday evening and informed him that they would be at Rem on Monday morning to change the locks on the doors and take over operations. On both occasions, no one showed up on Monday morning, and we simply went back to work as usual. We never called them for an explanation, and no explanation was ever given.

Our suppliers, on the other hand, continued to stand by us. They urged us to go ahead with the proposal. They had been selling to us on a cash basis for many months and expressed total confidence that, given the chance, Rem would survive and continue to do business with them. The suppliers continued to talk with each other and assured us that they would accept the proposal. So when the fateful day finally arrived when we met with all of our suppliers in Regina to find out if they would formally agree to forgive two-thirds of what Rem owed them, it was not a typical "bankruptcy" meeting.

For legal approval to go forward with our plan, we needed 85 percent agreement. With so much money on the line, we might have expected a great deal of heated discussion, but as it turned out, there were only a few questions, and the questions related to how Rem would treat the suppliers in the future. We later discovered through the court documents that this was the first time in the history of Saskatchewan that no one objected in such circumstances. All of our suppliers showed confidence that Rem would survive, and they looked forward to continuing to do business with Rem in the future.

In the following days, Helen and I reflected on our past together and how we had now been through a number of "bankruptcies." We married when I was twenty-one and Helen was eighteen. Soon after our wedding, when I was twenty-two, I recognized that I was spiritually bankrupt. I had "missed the mark" when it came to what God requires of us. I was overjoyed at that time to learn that Jesus Christ, God's Son, had paid the debt that I could never pay, and through repenting of my sins and acknowledging Him as my Lord, I could be forgiven and free. God's Word helped me to understand both my problem with sin and how to come out of my spiritual bankruptcy (see appendix 1).

Ten years later, at age thirty-two, I had faced a new bankruptcy. This one was physical. The carbon monoxide poisoning that occurred when I was working as a journeyman mechanic not only ended my mechanic career, it also almost destroyed my body. The boils, jaundice, and low blood pressure that followed were a long and painful trial. I had no strength during that time and was about as physically bankrupt as a person can be. Through fasting and prayer and a carrot juice diet, though, I eventually recovered. Soon I was able to work and pay the bills again, and I no longer had to count on friends buying groceries for my family. I came out of physical bankruptcy with a changed lifestyle and a new future as a cookware salesman.

Now, as I was approaching the age of sixty, I found myself financially bankrupt. Technically, bankruptcy is when secured creditors shut down a company and take over the assets, often selling them for a few cents on the dollar to recover as much of their loans as possible. Rem actually went through an "informal restructuring," which falls under the bankruptcy laws, where the secured creditors demand specific action in the hope that the company will survive and the creditors will fully recover their loans. In many ways, my financial "bankruptcy" was the most painful bankruptcy that I have faced. The company that we had built by God's grace and a lot of blood, sweat, and tears was on the verge of going under.

Although God had shown Stuart and me the way forward and given us favor with our suppliers and new investors, it would still take a decade to rebuild and become a family operated business once again. The financial uncertainty was very stressful during these years, but one of the most painful experiences was the loss of Stuart as my right-hand man in the fall of 1985 as he and Joellen followed God's leading for Stuart to pursue a new path in ministry. Also painful was the new status we carried as "bankrupt people," who were treated accordingly by some in our business community. It was a difficult time when hope was hard to cling to, but we gladly continued to walk by faith and trust the One who had always brought us through the bankruptcies of the past.

The new structure of Rem now included employees as major shareholders, with six of them holding key positions in the company. Under the terms set by our banker we operated under very strict rules. Every day was uncertain because the recession with its high interest rates continued. The new custom work we were doing did not prove to be immediately profitable. Worse yet, due to the startup costs involved and the need to learn new styles of production, we soon discovered a new threat to our survival, a threat that was heartbreaking for me as the founder of Rem, who had always put an emphasis on operating with integrity in all areas of the business. It came about after the first annual meeting of shareholders.

The launch of new product lines that we hoped would help Rem move forward in the uncertain economic times had still not produced profits for our new shareholders. No cash dividends could be paid if there were no profits. This was hard for some shareholders to understand, and it brought about tensions at the workplace. Rumors started circulating that Rem was not doing well. The new employee shareholders had access to a lot of information regarding our business operations, and they were searching for reasons for our lack of profits. Some discovered that we were still buying products from our former suppliers even though they were not always offering the lowest price. As this fact became known, it led to discontent. Instead of talking it over and finding out why we were buying from these particular suppliers, a few of our shareholder employees made efforts to remove me as president of the company.

It felt like my relational capital with my own employees was also entering into bankruptcy during this period, but despite the shock of my plunging popularity, I could not compromise what I considered to be our greatest asset, our integrity. I knew that our suppliers who had stood with us even when they suffered heavy losses were not always higher priced than other suppliers, and I was committed to not abandoning these businesses that had refused to abandon us in our time of need. I also knew that although our employee shareholders had not yet received a return on their investments in Rem, they all still had their jobs and were being paid regularly. Nevertheless, because I would not change our policy of relying on our former suppliers, I was now in danger of losing control of Rem, since I no longer had a controlling share in the company. Was this the end of our family business? It certainly looked that way—but the Lord had a different plan.

The first step of God's plan was revealed when Helen unexpectedly received an inheritance in cash. Around the same time, one of the ten employee shareholders needed to sell his 1 percent share in the company. Although the other nine had the first right to buy his share, they refused, showing their lack of confidence in the company's future. That refusal opened the door for Helen to purchase the 1 percent share after we had proven that the funds came from a private source rather than the company. That left Helen and me holding 39 percent of the Rem shares, still far short of having control of the company and protecting myself from losing my role as president, but God was not finished. As we have often found true, the Lord's ways are not our ways, and although God allowed us to regain control of Rem, it did not come about as we would have envisioned.

It was during this critical time that Stuart felt called to leave the company. Although I offered to be the one to leave so that Stuart could take over, the Lord had graciously made it very clear to Stuart about sixteen months earlier that his future was not with Rem. He had accepted this at the time and simply asked the Lord to show him when his time at Rem was up. Now the Lord had clearly done so, and when Stuart resigned he experienced incredible peace. He knew absolutely that the Lord was in control of both his life and the future of Rem, and he was ready for God's next assignment. He decided not only to resign but also to sell his 12 percent share in the company to me. He graciously asked for just one dollar up front and told me that I could pay him the remainder of the value of his shares if, when, and how I wanted, confident that I would be fair. As a result, Helen and I all of a sudden held 51 percent of the company's shares, and the struggle for control was over.

Throughout this time we were slowly buying back greater control of our company as shareholders decided to sell their shares. We still had the major challenge, though, of becoming a profitable company once again. The product line that had led us to expand our business and that we were relying on to carry us into the new decade was very slow to recover. This led us to put more energy into pursuing custom work, which ultimately led us to what is still the most profitable product line of Rem today. Here's how it happened.

Rem had begun as a chaff blower manufacturing company. We soon added a vacuum feed blower, and then we began to supply our customers with more efficient high-pressure blowers for air seeders. As I mentioned in the previous chapter, we found in the early 1980s that one of our customers was buying our blowers and using them as part of a "cleanup vac" he was trying to design. When he ended up with a terminal illness, he agreed to sell his patent and producing rights to me. We then redesigned this machine, and in 1984, the first year as a newly restructured company, we began to build our first grain vac. It was a costly new venture, which made the new shareholders nervous, but sales increased for this grain vac each year, and Rem was showing signs of moving toward being profitable again.

Although the upturn in sales still did not put us in a position to buy out the remaining shareholders, we found another way. As we had some profitable years, we were able to begin making improvements on the eighty-acre farm we had purchased in 1979. This helped increase the property's value considerably and made it possible for us to take out a mortgage on the farm to buy back the remaining Rem shares that were held by others. And so, six years after the restructuring, we were able to buy out the remaining shareholders, and all of them were very pleased with their earnings. In fact, when I paid the last shareholder off, I asked if he was satisfied with the return on his investment. He responded that he had earned more on his investment than he had ever done before and wondered how I could afford such a good return.

The shareholder years were finally behind us. Now we were free to operate as a family business, as we had originally intended. We asked ourselves how a family business committed to integrity should deal with the suppliers who had helped us when the business was on the verge of closing. The answer was clear, and we began to follow up with each one of them that had taken a loss as a result of our informal restructuring. Although there were one or two smaller accounts that we could not find, we tried our best to contact all of the suppliers, and we made certain that our accounts were settled in a satisfactory way.

I remember contacting Stelco, a spring wire company that had suffered the greatest loss when they agreed to take thirty-four cents on the dollar for what we had owed them. When I asked them, though, what I still owed them, the manager replied, "You've been buying millions of dollars of steel from us since the 'bankruptcy,' and we haven't been giving you discounts. You don't owe us anything, and we are pleased that you're still buying our steel."

About eight years later, I received a letter from another supplier, telling us, "We've charged you a little bit extra, at times, and haven't given you a cash discount. We added up these factors, and you don't owe us anything. And from now on, we'll give you a cash discount once again." By staying with these suppliers, even though their prices were a bit higher without the cash discount we could have gotten elsewhere, we were able to not only survive as a company but also act with integrity toward those who had helped us at our greatest time of need.

When the decade of trials was finally behind us, a friend who is ten years younger than me said, "I also went bankrupt in the early 1980s in my farming operation, and I still haven't recovered. Now I feel like an old man." He then asked, "How do you feel after what you've been through?"

I replied, "Our 'bankruptcy' was the best thing that could have happened to me; I learned a lot of lessons through the many struggles we faced." The most important lesson that Helen and I learned was to invest our energy in staying close to God. He is the Vine, and we are the branches. If we are not actively staying connected to Him, we will never get the nourishment we need. Working hard to stay close to God is particularly important during those periods when we need even more nourishment than usual to survive and grow. As we learned to rely more and more on God, Helen and I discovered just how true the words of the old hymn by Annie Johnson Flint are ("He Giveth More Grace"):

> *He giveth more strength as our burdens grow greater,*
> *He sendeth more strength as our labors increase;*
> *To added afflictions He addeth His mercy,*
> *To multiplied trials He multiplies peace.*

> *His love has no limit, His grace has no measure,*
> *His power no boundary known unto men;*
> *For out of His infinite riches in Jesus*
> *He giveth, and giveth, and giveth again.*

CHAPTER XXI

A New Millennium and New Beginnings

As the new millennium arrived, growing demand for our products brought with it a variety of challenges. In response, we began taking greater advantage of new computer technology, software, and high speed Internet. We also embarked on a complete overhaul of our approach to drafting, with our engineers learning how to do 3D computer drafting. We had come a long way since introducing the first IBM personal computer at Rem in 1984. All of this significantly helped us both to improve production and to expand our global marketing efforts.

Over the years, our exports to the U.S. had continued to expand. As we moved into the first decade of the new millennium we became convinced that establishing a site in the U.S. would improve our ability to serve that market. We began by purchasing a warehouse in Fargo, North Dakota, near our top U.S. sales representative. That was a step forward, but we wondered about actually doing some of our manufacturing south of the border. In 2005, we decided to establish a factory in Shenandoah, Iowa. The factory opened the following year; another new adventure had begun.

In 2000, our daughter Donna Jane had called and said that she was very sick and wanted to come home. I told her, "Come gladly." Then she told me that her husband, Bob, would like to work at Rem. I told her to give me some time to think and pray about it.

Opening the new factory in Shenandoah, Iowa, 2006

It was Indian summer, and we had been seeking the Lord for about a month. There was a thick layer of yellow leaves on the ground in our yard as I walked along talking to the Lord. "Lord, I need to know, is it Your will to have Bob come and work at Rem?" There came a still, small voice—a strong sense of inner peace—that afternoon.

A few days later, I called Jane and said, "Why don't you and Bob come and visit? We'll talk about the job and coming home to the farm." I told her that the business had grown and the challenges were much larger now. I said that a family business cannot survive unless it has a clear value system. Those in leadership need to show support and confidence in each other and have a unity of purpose that everyone adheres to. I wanted them to understand how committed I was to running Rem as our Father's business. I also wanted them to know that we had a place ready for them to live in. We wanted not only to be quick to use the resources God entrusted to us to fulfill the Great Commission, but also to meet needs in our own family as they arose.

When they arrived, Bob and I discussed very briefly the major items that were important to us. We had had some differences in the past, but neither of us needed to bring those up again. As Bob came on board, the two of us, together with Leann, Helen, and Jane, began to sort out and hire new accounting and sales personnel and develop a strong marketing plan, especially for the U.S. market. For the spiritual health of our employees, we remained committed to our outreach program, and we saw good results. We began an Alpha program at lunchtime and found that it was an important ministry to some of our employees.

We had started bringing Filipinos to Swift Current in 2006 after studying the potential of bringing in foreign workers. Though it took a lot of time, work, and planning, they have been hardworking and loyal employees, and many of them came to know or grow in the Lord through our ministries at Rem.

Receiving my honorary Doctor of Divinity Degree from President Dwayne Uglem at Briercrest College and Seminary, 2009

The Rem team, 2011

Epilogue

At the foundation of all of our ministry involvement over the years was our commitment to the business God had called us to build. Whether serving on Millar's board, working with Campus Crusade, helping out in short-term missions, or working at Rem, we wanted to be about our Father's business. Many years ago, as I sought to be a branch that would bear much fruit, I thought that I would have to be involved in full-time ministry. God made it clear, though, that He had other ideas. He called me to be a businessman and to use the wealth that He entrusted to us through our business in whatever way He directed. He, of course, also gave Helen and me countless opportunities to serve in various ministry roles, but we came to understand that our roles at Rem and in our own family were equally part of being about our Father's business.

Jesus said, "Whoever has my commands and obeys them, he is the one who loves me. He who loves me will be loved by my Father, and I too will love him and show myself to him" (John 14:21). We love God by finding out what is pleasing to Him (Ephesians 5:10) and then making the choice to do it. The more we choose to live in obedience to God, the more fruitful we are, and the more abundant our lives are as He shows Himself to us.

We have had the joy of seeing God powerfully at work in countless different situations as we have chosen to seek first His kingdom and His righteousness. Nothing could be better than a life about our Father's business. Nothing could be better than living as a branch connected to the Vine, one day at a time.

We hope and pray that as our children, grandchildren, and others hear our story of learning to live by faith they will be encouraged to love and follow the Lord with all their hearts, souls, minds, and strength. From beginning to end, God has been faithful to us. He has patiently taught us His ways, forgiven us when we failed, strengthened us when we were weak, and graciously allowed us to be tools in His hands to minister to others. He has never been anything other than completely faithful. Through it all, He has taught us that life is not about us; it's about honoring Him and helping others to know Him personally.

Having gone from living with next to nothing to having far more than we need, it would be easy to get caught up in the pursuit of wealth. Instead, God has helped us to focus on storing up treasure in heaven rather than on earth. He has directed us time and time again to use the money that He has entrusted to us to meet a need or to advance His kingdom—His money for His purposes. With whatever years and resources God entrusts to us in the future, our sole desire is to continue to be about our Father's business.

Frank Rempel

Have You Made the Most Important Choice of Your Life?

L ife is all about choices. Whether it's what to eat, where to live, or what to do for a career, we all face many choices throughout our lives. One choice, though, is far more important than any of the others. I hope you have seen that clearly through this book, but I want to emphasize how important it is. Had I not made this choice, my life would have been dramatically different. In fact, I would not have had life at all! Let me explain.

The Bible teaches that "There is no one righteous, not even one" (Romans 3:10) and "all have sinned and fall short of the glory of God" (Romans 3:23). In other words, we have all fallen short of God's perfect standards. There are no exceptions. We are all in the same boat! Plain and simple, there really is no such thing as a "good person." We like to think that we're better than the guy next door, but unfortunately God doesn't compare us to others; He compares us to Himself and His standards. And the reality is that when we compare ourselves to a holy God, the degree to which sin has infected us is shocking. Our very best doesn't even come close to reaching God's standards. In fact, He says that "all our righteous acts are like filthy rags" (Isaiah 64:6).

How can God say this? How can He view the good things that we do as being no more valuable than a rag soaked in filth? Think about it for a minute. Suppose you murdered someone and are standing trial before a judge. There's no question in anyone's mind that you committed the crime. In fact, you readily admit that you did it. To defend yourself, though, you draw the judge's attention to a long list of good things you've done throughout your life. You've been very generous in taking care of the people around you, including strangers. You've helped many people. You are a good person! Surely that should outweigh the one crime you committed. And so you ask the judge to find you "not guilty" because of the good deeds you have done.

What do you think the judge is going to say? Is he going to put your good deeds on the scale and see if they outweigh the brutal murder you committed? No! He is going to punish you for the crime you committed because He is a just judge.

God is also a just judge, and He *must* punish sin. The Bible makes it clear that "the wages of sin [the punishment or penalty for sin] is death" (Romans 6:23). This death is not just physical death; it is a one-way ticket to the Lake of Fire, otherwise known as hell (see Revelation 20:12–15). That's Bad News, and we rightly tremble at what is in store for us!

But despite these facts, there is hope. There is hope because there is Good News! The Good News is that although we have sinned against God, *He* has taken steps to rescue us from the horrible judgment awaiting us. So although all of us deserve God's punishment in hell, and God, being just, must carry out our sentence, He has made a way of escape and given us a choice: we can choose to suffer the punishment we deserve ourselves or have someone else pay the penalty for us. And that is exactly what Jesus came to do!

The Bible tells us that Jesus has always existed (see John 1:1). He Himself is God, and through Him all things were created (see John 1:3). And yet Jesus, the Son of God, chose to become a human being to carry out God's rescue operation (see John 1:14). He lived like you and I live; He faced the same kinds of temptations that we face; but He never ever sinned (Hebrews 4:15). Because He was both God and man and had absolutely no sin, He was able to pay the price for the sins of *all* those who belong to Him. Did you hear that? Jesus satisfied God's justice! Jesus died in your place and in my place, if we belong to Him.

But not everyone embraces what Jesus has done for them. Remember, Jesus has satisfied God's justice for *those who belong to Him*. What does it mean to belong to Him? How can we belong to Him?

The answer is actually quite simple, but also quite serious. Listen to what the Bible says: "If you declare with your mouth, 'Jesus is Lord,' and believe in your heart that God raised him from the dead, you will be saved" (Romans 10:9). Saved from what? Saved from the penalty of your sins. Saved from eternity in hell. But two things are necessary.

First, we must believe what God has done for us through Jesus. Jesus died on the cross, bearing the penalty for our sins, and God raised Him from the dead three days later. Through His death our sins are paid for; through His resurrection we have the promise of new life now and of eternal life when this life is over. God asks us to believe this, but He also requires something else. He requires that we confess that "Jesus is Lord." What does that mean?

The Good News is both an announcement of what Jesus has done *for* us and an urgent call for us to respond *to* Him. To confess that Jesus is Lord is to give our allegiance to Him. It is like surrendering to a more powerful army and declaring, "You're the boss. I will serve You from this day forward." To acknowledge that Jesus is Lord is to renounce any claim I have to being my own master. It is to turn from my old way of life and begin living *for Him*. So, becoming a Christian—that is, one who belongs to Jesus and has thus been rescued from the terrible fate awaiting humankind—is not a minor decision; it is a decision that will affect every area of your life.

You see, salvation is a gift from God. There is nothing we can do to earn it for ourselves. But it requires that we embrace Jesus as our Lord. It is thus free, but not without implications and obligations. Quite the contrary. Becoming one who belongs to Jesus means leaving your old life behind. It's much like joining the military. It doesn't cost you anything to get in, but if you join, someone else will tell you when to get up, what to wear, what to eat, what hairstyle you will have, etc. *Everything* changes.

When we surrender our life to Jesus, the Bible tells us that God adopts us into His family. We become His child! He will now love us and care for us as a Father, and we are to live to bring honor to our Father's name. When we surrender our life to Jesus, the Bible tells us that we become citizens of the Kingdom of Heaven, His kingdom. Now we must live by the values of that kingdom. We no longer belong to ourselves; Jesus has purchased us for Himself with His own blood (see 1 Corinthians 6:19–20).

The fact that everything changes when we make the decision to belong to Jesus is one of the reasons Jesus commands His followers to be baptized. Baptism—basically having your body dunked under water and then raised back up—is a picture of being buried and then raised from the dead. It vividly symbolizes that your old life is over. That person you were has died. You are a new person now! It also symbolizes that your sins have been washed away. And the fact that you are baptized in the name of the Father, Son, and Holy Spirit means that you now belong to God.

To turn to God, you must turn from sin. The Bible calls this "repentance," and it's a choice that we must all make. When we make this choice, the Bible says that we are "born again." It's not just that a new life begins; it's much more than that. We are actually changed to the very depth of our beings. We go from having hearts that make us God's enemies to having new hearts that actually desire to please God. God puts His Holy Spirit within us and begins utterly transforming our lives. He begins making us like Jesus, and as He does so we experience life more and more as He intended it to be, an "abundant life."

This does not mean that life becomes easy; indeed, Christians face many trials, some of which come precisely because they are followers of Jesus. But through the challenges of life God is with us, giving us the strength to persevere through the trials, knowing that we have a wonderful inheritance awaiting us in His presence in heaven.

Today, if you are still an enemy of God, estranged from Him because of your sins, choose to believe what Jesus has done for you and confess "Jesus is Lord." If you do that, you will be saved, saved from the ultimate penalty of your sins, and also set free and empowered to live life today as God intended, enjoying an intimate relationship with the God of the universe.

If it is your desire to choose life through Jesus today, you can pray the following prayer. Then, as one who now belongs to Jesus, be sure to find a church where the Bible is taught accurately and be baptized there and become a part of that local family of believers.

Dear God,
Today I humbly bow before You in gratitude for what You have done
for me through Jesus Christ, Your Son. I believe that Jesus came to

earth and lived as a man, died as a sinless sacrifice on the cross to pay the penalty of my sins, and was raised from the dead so that I might have life through Him. I choose to turn from my sins today and gladly confess that Jesus is my Lord. I choose to follow Him, to belong to Him, to live my life to please my new Master. Please give me a new heart and fill me with Your Holy Spirit as You have promised to do for all those who belong to You. Amen.

If you need help finding a solid church, we suggest contacting one of the churches listed in the Gospel Coalition Church Directory: http://thegospelcoalition.org/network/church-directory/

APPENDIX 2

Have You Made the Wonderul Discovery of the Spirit-Filled Life?

Every day can be an exciting adventure for the Christian who knows the reality of being filled with the Holy Spirit and who lives constantly, moment by moment, under His gracious direction.

The Bible tells us that there are three kinds of people:

1. NATURAL PERSON

(One who has not received Christ) "A natural man does not accept the things of the

Self-Directed Life
S – Self is on the throne
✝ – Christ is outside the life
● – Interests are directed by self, often resulting in discord and frustration

Spirit of God; for they are foolishness to him, and he cannot understand them, because they are spiritually appraised" (1 Corinthians 2:14).

2. SPIRITUAL PERSON

(One who is directed and empowered by the Holy Spirit) "He who is spiritual appraises all things...

Christ-Directed Life
✝ – Christ is in the life and on the throne
S – Self is yielding to Christ
● – Interests are directed by Christ, resulting in harmony with God's plan

We have the mind of Christ" (1-Corinthians 2:15,16).

3. WORLDLY (CARNAL) PERSON

(One who has received Christ, but who lives in defeat because he is trying to live the Christian-life in his own strength)

Self-Directed Life
S – Self is on the throne
† – Christ dethroned and not allowed to direct the life
● – Interests are directed by self, often resulting in discord and frustration

"Brothers, I could not address you as spiritual but as worldly—mere infants in Christ. I gave you milk, not solid food, for you were not yet ready for it. Indeed, you are still not ready. You are still worldly. For since there is jealousy and quarreling among you, are you not worldly? Are you not acting like mere men?" (1 Corinthians 3:1–3, NIV).

The following are four principles for living the Spirit-filled life.

 God has provided for us an abundant and fruitful Christian life.

Jesus said, "I have come that they may have life, and that they may have it more abundantly" (John 10:10, NKJ).

"I am the vine, you are the branches. He who abides in Me, and I in him, bears much fruit; for without Me you can do nothing" (John 15:5, NKJ).

"The fruit of the Spirit is love, joy, peace, patience, kindness, goodness, faithfulness, gentleness, self-control; against such things there is no law" (Galatians 5:22,23).

"You shall receive power when the Holy Spirit has come upon you; and you shall be My witnesses both in Jerusalem, and in all Judea and Samaria, and even to the remotest part of the earth" (Acts 1:8).

The following are some personal traits of the spiritual person
that result from trusting God:

- Love
- Joy
- Peace
- Patience
- Kindness
- Faithfulness
- Goodness

- Life is Christ-centered
- Empowered by Holy Spirit
- Introduces others to Christ
- Has effective prayer life
- Understands God's Word
- Trusts God
- Obeys God

The degree to which these traits are manifested in the life
depends on the extent to which the Christian trusts the
Lord with every detail of his life, and on his maturity in
Christ. One who is only beginning to understand the ministry of the Holy Spirit should not be discouraged if he is
not as fruitful as more mature Christians who have known
and experienced this truth for a longer period.

*Why is it that most Christians are not experiencing the abundant
life?*

 **Worldly Christians cannot experience the
abundant and fruitful-Christian life.**

The worldly (carnal) person trusts in his own efforts to live
the Christian life:

◆ He is either uninformed about, or has forgotten, God's
love, forgiveness, and power (Romans 5:8–10; Hebrews
10:1–25; 1 John 1; 2:1–3; 2-Peter 1:9; Acts-1:8).

◆ He has an up-and-down spiritual experience.

◆ He cannot understand himself—he wants to do what is
right, but cannot.

◆ He fails to draw on the power of the Holy Spirit to live
the Christian life (1-Corinthians 3:1–3; Romans 7:15–24;
8:7; Galatians 5:16–18).

Some or all of the following traits may characterize the worldly person—the Christian who does not fully trust God: (The individual who professes to be a Christian but who

- Legalistic attitude
- Impure thoughts
- Jealousy
- Guilt
- Worry
- Discouragement
- Critical spirit
- Frustration
- Aimlessness

- Fear
- Ignorance of his spiritual heritage
- Unbelief
- Disobedience
- Loss of love for God and for others
- Poor prayer life
- No desire for Bible study

continues to practice sin should realize that he may not be a Christian at all, according to 1 John 2:3; 3:6–9; Ephesians 5:5.)

The third truth gives us the only solution to this problem...

 Jesus promised the abundant and fruitful life as-the result of being filled (directed and empowered) by the Holy Spirit.

The Spirit-filled life is the Christ-directed life by which Christ lives His life in and through us in the power of the Holy Spirit (John 15).

◆ One becomes a Christian through the ministry of the Holy Spirit, according to John 3:1–8. From the moment of spiritual birth, the Christian is indwelt by the Holy Spirit at all times (John 1:12; Colossians 2:9,10; John 14:16,17).

Though all Christians are indwelt by the Holy Spirit, not all Christians are filled (directed and empowered) by the Holy Spirit on an ongoing basis.

◆ The Holy Spirit is the source of the overflowing life (John 7:37–39).

◆ The Holy Spirit came to glorify Christ (John 16:1–15). When one is filled with the Holy Spirit, he is a true disciple of Christ.

◆ In His last command before His ascension, Christ promised the power-of the Holy Spirit to enable us to be witnesses for Him (Acts-1:1–9).

How, then, can one be filled with the Holy Spirit?

 We are filled with the Holy Spirit by faith; then we-can experience the abundant and fruitful life-that Christ promised.

You can appropriate the filling of the Holy Spirit **right now** if you:

◆ Sincerely desire to be directed and empowered by the Holy Spirit (Matthew 5:6; John 7:37–39).

◆ Confess your sins. By **faith**, thank God that He **has** forgiven all of your sins—past, present, and future— because Christ died for you (Colossians 2:13–15; 1 John 1; 2:1–3; Hebrews 10:1–17).

◆ Present every area of your life to God (Romans 12:1,2).

173

◆ By **faith** claim the fullness of the Holy Spirit, according to:

His command: Be filled with the Spirit.

"Do not get drunk on wine, which leads to debauchery. Instead, be filled with the Spirit" (Ephesians 5:18, NIV).

His promise: He will always answer when we pray according to His-will.

"This is the confidence we have in approaching God: that if we ask anything according to his will, he hears us. And if we know that He hears us—whatever we ask—we know that we have what we asked of Him" (1 John 5:14,15, NIV).

Faith can be expressed through prayer…

How to Pray in Faith to be Filled With the Holy Spirit

We are filled with the Holy Spirit by **faith** alone. However, true prayer is one way of expressing our faith. The following is a suggested prayer:

> Dear Father, I need You. I acknowledge that I have sinned against You by directing my own life. I thank You that You have forgiven my sins through Christ's death on the cross for me. I now invite Christ to again take His place on the throne of my life. Fill me with the Holy Spirit as You **commanded** me to be filled, and as You **promised** in Your Word that You would do if I asked in faith. I pray this in the name of Jesus. As an expression of my faith, I now thank You for directing my life and for filling me with the Holy Spirit.

Does this prayer express the desire of your heart? If so, bow in prayer and trust God to fill you with the Holy Spirit **right now**.

How to Know That You Are Filled
(Directed and Empowered) By the Holy Spirit

Did you ask God to fill you with the Holy Spirit? Do you know that you are now filled with the Holy Spirit? On what authority? (On the trustworthiness of God Himself and His Word: Hebrews 11:6; John 17:17.)

Do not depend on feelings. The promise of God's Word, not our feelings, is our-authority. The Christian lives by faith (trust) in the trustworthiness of God Himself and His Word. This train diagram illustrates the relationship among **fact** (God and His Word), **faith** (our trust in God and His Word), and **feeling** (the result of our faith and obedience) (John 14:21).

The train will run with or without the caboose. However, it-would be futile to

attempt to pull the train by the caboose. In the same way, we as Christians do not depend on feelings or emotions, but we place our faith (trust)-in the trustworthiness of God and the promises of His Word.

13

How to Walk in the Spirit

Faith (trust in God and His promises) is the only way a Christian can live the Spirit-directed life. As you continue to trust Christ moment by moment:

◆ Your life will demonstrate more and more of the fruit of the Spirit (Galatians 5:22,23) and will be more and more conformed to the image of Christ (Romans 12:2; 2 Corinthians 3:18).

◆ Your prayer life and study of God's Word will become more meaningful.

◆ You will experience His power in witnessing (Acts 1:8).

◆ You will be prepared for spiritual conflict against the world (1 John 2:15–17); against the flesh (Galatians 5:16,17); and against Satan (1-Peter-5:7–9; Ephesians 6:10–13).

◆ You will experience His power to resist temptation and sin (1 Corinthians 10:13; Philippians 4:13; Ephesians 1:19–23; 2 Timothy 1:7; Romans 6:1–16).

Spiritual Breathing

If you become aware of an area of your life (an attitude or an action) that is displeasing to the Lord, even though you are walking with Him and sincerely desiring to serve Him, simply thank God that He has forgiven your sins—past, present, and future—on the basis of Christ's death on the cross. Claim His love and forgiveness by-faith and continue to have fellowship with Him.

If you retake the throne of your life through sin—a definite act of disobedience—breathe spiritually. Spiritual Breathing (exhaling the impure and inhaling the pure) is-an exercise in faith that enables you to experience God's love and forgiveness.

1. *Exhale:* Confess your sin—agree with God concerning your sin and thank Him for-His forgiveness of it, according to 1 John 1:9 and Hebrews 10:1–25. Confession involves repentance—a change in attitude and action.

2. *Inhale:* Surrender the control of your life to Christ, and receive the-fullness of-the-Holy Spirit by faith. Trust that He now directs and empowers you, according to-the **command** of Ephesians 5:18 and the **promise** of 1 John 5:14,15.

If this booklet has been helpful to you, please share it with someone else.

To encourage the widest distribution possible, this booklet is available at a nominal price for use by you or your organization. You may place your name or the name of your organization in the space below.

Written by Bill Bright. © 2008 Bright Media Foundation and Campus Crusade for Christ. Formerly © 1966, 1995, 2000, Campus Crusade for Christ, Inc. All rights reserved. No part of this booklet may be changed in any way or reproduced in any form without written permission from Campus Crusade for Christ. Published by New Life Resources, 375 Hwy 74 South, Suite A, Peachtree City, GA 30269.

EAN13 978-1-56399-020-5

CAMPUS CRUSADE FOR CHRIST
Building Spiritual Movements Everywhere

375 Hwy 74 South, Suite A
Peachtree City, GA 30269
www.campuscrusde.org
800-827-2788